Engaging God's Word

Deuteronomy

Engage Bible Studies

Tools That Transform

Engage Bible Studies

an imprint of

COMMUNITY
BIBLE STUDY

Engaging God's Word: Deuteronomy
Copyright © 2013 by Community Bible Study. All rights reserved.
ISBN 978-1-62194-019-7

Published by Community Bible Study
790 Stout Road
Colorado Springs, CO 80921-3802
1-800-826-4181
www.communitybiblestudy.org

Printed in the United States of America.

Contents

Introduction

Welcome to the life-changing adventure of engaging with God's Word! Whether this is the first time you've opened a Bible or you've studied the Scriptures all your life, good things are in store for you. Studying the Bible is unlike any other kind of study you have ever done. That's because the Word of God is *"living and active"* (Hebrews 4:12) and transcends time and cultures. The earth and heavens as we know them will one day pass away, but God's Word never will (Mark 13:31). It's as relevant to your life today as it was to the people who wrote it down centuries ago. And the fact that God's Word is living and active means that reading God's Word is always meant to be a personal experience. God's Word is not just dead words on a page—it is page after page of living, powerful words—so get ready, because the time you spend studying the Bible in this *Engaging God's Word* course will be life-transforming!

Why Study the Bible?

Some Christians read the Bible because they know they're supposed to. It's a good thing to do, and God expects it. And all that's true! However, there are many additional reasons to study God's Word. Here are just some of them.

We get to know God through His Word. Our God is a relational God who knows us and wants us to know Him. The Scriptures, which He authored, reveal much about Him: how He thinks and feels, what His purposes are, what He thinks about us, how He views the world He made, what He has planned for the future. The Bible shows us God's many attributes—His kindness, goodness, justice, love, faithfulness, mercy, compassion, creativity, redemption, sovereignty, and so on. As we get to know Him through His Word, we come to love and trust Him.

God speaks to us through His Word. One of the primary ways God speaks to us is through His written Word. Don't be surprised if, as you read the Bible, certain parts nearly jump off the page at you, almost as if they'd been written with you in mind. God is the Author of this incredible book, so that's not just possible, it's likely! Whether it is to find comfort, warning, correction, teaching, or guidance, always approach God's Word with your spiritual ears open (Isaiah 55:3) because God, your loving heavenly Father, has things He wants to say to you.

God's Word brings life. Just about everyone wants to learn the secret to "the good life." And the good news is, that secret is found in God's Word. Don't think of the Bible as a bunch of rules. Viewing it with that mindset is a distortion. God gave us His Word because as our Creator and the Creator of the universe, He alone knows how life was meant to work. He knows that love makes us happier than hate, that generosity brings more joy than greed, and that integrity allows us to rest more peacefully at night than deception does. God's ways are not always "easiest," but they are the way to life. As the Psalmist says, *"If Your law had not been my delight, I would have perished in my affliction. I will never forget Your precepts, for by them You have given me life"* (Psalm 119:92-93).

God's Word offers stability in an unstable world. Truth is an ever-changing negotiable for many people in our culture today. But building your life on constantly changing "truth" is like building your house on shifting sand. God's Word, like God Himself, never changes. What He says was true yesterday. It is true today. And it will still be true a billion years from now. Jesus said, *"Everyone then who hears these words of Mine and does them will be like a wise man who built his house on the rock"* (Matthew 7:24).

God's Word helps us to pray effectively. When we read God's Word and get to know what He is really like, we understand better how to pray. God answers prayers that are according to His will. We discover His will by reading the Bible. First John 5:14-15 tells us that *"this is the confidence that we have toward Him, that if we ask anything according to His will He hears us. And if we know that He hears us in whatever we ask, we know that we have the requests that we have asked of Him."*

How to Get the Most out of *Engaging God's Word*

Each *Engaging God's Word* study contains key elements that have been carefully designed to help you get the most out of your time in God's Word. Slightly modified for your study-at-home success, this approach is very similar to the tried-and-proven Bible study method that Community Bible Study has used with thousands of men, women, and children across the United States and around the world for nearly 40 years. There are some basic things you can expect to find in each course in this series.

❖ Lesson 1 provides an overview of the Bible book (or books) you will study and questions to help you focus, anticipate, and pray about what you will be learning.

❖ Every lesson contains questions to answer on your own, commentary that reviews and clarifies the passage, and three special sections called "Apply what you have learned," "Think about," and "Personalize this lesson."

❖ Some lessons contain memory verse suggestions.

Whether you plan to use *Engaging God's Word* on your own or with a group, here are some suggestions that will help you enjoy and receive the most benefit from your study.

Spread out each lesson over several days. Your *Engaging God's Word* lessons were designed to take a week to complete. Spreading out your study rather than doing it all at once allows time for the things God is teaching you to sink in and for you to practice applying them.

Pray each time you read God's Word. The Bible is a book unlike any other because God Himself inspired it. The same Spirit who inspired the human authors who wrote it will help you to understand and apply it if you ask Him to. So make it a practice to ask Him to make His Word come alive to you every time you read it.

Read the whole passage covered in the lesson. Before plunging into the questions, take time to read the specific chapter or verses that will be covered in that lesson. Doing this will give you important context for the whole lesson. Reading the Bible in context is an important principle in interpreting it accurately.

Begin learning the memory verse. Learning Scripture by heart requires discipline, but the rewards far outweigh the effort. Memorizing a verse allows you to recall it whenever you need it—for personal encouragement and direction, or to share with someone else. Consider writing the verse on a sticky note or index card that you can post where you will see it often or carry with you to review during the day. Reading and re-reading the verse often—out loud when possible—is a simple way to commit it to memory.

Re-read the passage for each section of questions. Each lesson is divided into sections so that you study one small part of Scripture at a time. Before attempting to answer the questions, review the verses that the questions will cover.

Answer the questions without consulting the Commentary or other reference materials. There is great joy in having the Holy Spirit teach you God's Word on your own, without the help of outside resources. Don't cheat yourself of the delight of discovery by reading the Commentary prematurely. Wait until after you've completed the lesson.

Repeat the process for all the question sections.

Prayerfully consider the "Apply what you have learned," marked with the 📌 push pin symbol. The vision of Community Bible Study is not just to gain knowledge about the Bible, but to be transformed by it. For this reason, each set of questions closes with a section that encourages you to apply what you are learning. Usually this section involves action—something for you to do. As you practice these suggestions, your life will change.

Read the Commentary. *Engaging God's Word* commentaries are written by theologians whose goal is to help you understand the context of what you are studying as it relates to the rest of Scripture, God's character, and what the passage means for your life. Of necessity, the commentaries include the author's interpretations. While interesting and helpful, keep in mind that the Commentary is simply one person's understanding of what these passages mean. Other godly men and women have views that are also worth considering.

Pause to contemplate each "Think about" section, marked with the ☐ notepad symbol. These features, embedded in the Commentary, offer a place to pause and consider some of the principles being brought out by the text. They provide excellent ideas to journal about or to discuss with other believers, especially those doing the study with you.

Jot down insights or prayer points from the "Personalize this lesson" marked with the ☑ check box symbol. While the "Apply what you have learned" section focuses on doing, the "Personalize this lesson" section focuses on becoming. Spiritual transformation is not just about doing right things and refraining from doing wrong things—it is about changing from the inside out. To be transformed means letting God change our hearts so that our attitudes, emotions, desires, reactions, and goals are increasingly like Jesus'. Often this section will discuss something that you cannot do in your own strength—so your response will usually be something to pray about. Remember that becoming more Christ-like is not just a matter of trying harder—it requires God's empowerment.

God Is Ever Faithful
Deuteronomy

As we navigate life in the 21st century with all of its uncertainties and stress, how can we know without a doubt that God is on our side? By studying Deuteronomy, you will gain insight into His faithfulness and encouragement for your journey in this fallen world. Our God promises to find us in the wilderness, to rescue and preserve us, and to guide us with His Word (32:10-12).

Moses *"the man of God"* (33:1) wrote the book of Deuteronomy. He reminded the Israelites of God's constant faithfulness and love as they hesitated fearfully on the border of the land promised to Abraham and his descendants long ago. Moses exhorted the Israelites to *"remember and do not forget"* (9:7) everything God had already done to rescue them from slavery and to sustain them through nearly 40 years of desert wandering. In response, Israel needed to step forward courageously in faith and obedience.

Likewise, we need to remember His grace and respond with obedience as we *"stand … before the* LORD [our] *God"* (29:10). God chose us *"to be a people for His treasured possession"* simply because He loves us (7:6). The Lord desires for us to fear Him (10:20), to walk in His ways (11:22), to love Him (11:1), to serve Him (10:20), and to obey Him always (11:8). In return, God promises His faithfulness will not waver—despite our faithlessness.

We need to choose. We can choose the temporary pleasures of this world, or we can *"choose life … loving the* LORD *your God, obeying His voice and holding fast to Him"* (30:19-20) as we look forward to life eternal with Him.

Just as Moses and his successor Joshua bravely and courageously led Israel, we need to bravely claim the *"land"* God sets before us in our lives (1:21). He loves us, He encourages us, He cares for us, He sustains us, He guides us, and He is ever faithful.

Will you choose to walk in God's ways and *"Rejoice before the LORD your God in all that you undertake"* (12:18)? God truly is your *"Rock"* (32:4), and He *"fights for you"* (3:22) every day of your life. In response to His gracious love and redemption through His Son Jesus Christ, will you choose to lean into Him and to obey Him? In return, He will bless you with His perfect peace throughout the joys and hardships of your life.

1. The Israelites wandered through the wilderness long after God delivered them from slavery in Egypt. Have you experienced "wilderness" years in your life? If so, how have you responded?

     _____

     _____

     _____

2. What has God done in your life that you want to remember and not forget?

     _____

     _____

     _____

3. What does it mean to you to walk in His ways and to serve Him?

     _____

     _____

     _____

If you are doing this study as a group, take time to pray for one another about your answers to these questions. Ask God to reveal truth to you and to increase your trust in Him as you do this study. If you are studying by yourself, write your prayer in the space below.

Lesson 2

Israel, God's People
Deuteronomy 1–3

Memorize God's Word: Deuteronomy 3:22.

❖ Deuteronomy 1:1-18—God's Command

1. Read Deuteronomy 1:5 and 34:1. Where are Moses and God's people?

   _____

   _____

   _____

2. As Moses begins his address to the Israelites, he tells them to *"take possession of the land that the Lord swore to your fathers ... to give them and to their offspring"* (Deuteronomy 1:8). If God gave it to them, then why did they have to take it?

   _____

   _____

   _____

   _____

3. How do the events recorded in Deuteronomy begin to fulfill the promise of Genesis 12:2-3? (See also Genesis 13:14-17.)

   _____

   _____

   _____

   _____

4. What does Moses remind the people about in Deuteronomy 1:9-18? Who had advised Moses to take this action, and why? (See Exodus 18.)

    _____

    _____

    _____

5. What, according to Moses, is required of Israel's judges (1:16-18)?

    _____

    _____

❖ Deuteronomy 1:19-46—A Crisis and Its Consequences

6. What was Moses' reply to the previous generation's protests that the Promised Land's current inhabitants were too strong for them?

    _____

    _____

    _____

7. When the people persisted in their unbelief and fear, how did God finally respond?

    _____

    _____

8. Who were the exceptions?

    _____

    _____

9. Why did God bar Moses from entering the Promised Land? (See Numbers 20, particularly verses 11-12.)

    _____

    _____

    _____

10. As a believer, what can you learn from this?

_____

_____

_____

11. Do you think God acted harshly, or was His decision consistent with His character? Or both?

_____

_____

_____

12. How did the Israelites respond to God's evident anger?

_____

_____

13. What happened to them?

_____

_____

_____

❖ Deuteronomy 2:1-25—Wilderness Years

14. Who will the Israelites encounter as they pass through Seir? How do Genesis 27 and 28 add to your understanding of these people?

_____

_____

_____

15. Next, the Israelites encountered the Moabites and the Ammonites. What does Genesis 19:36-38 reveal about these tribes?

_____

_____

_____

❖ Deuteronomy 2:26–3:29—Conquest and Possession of the Promised Land

16. Moses says God made Sihon's heart obstinate as part of His plan. How does the story of Pharaoh's hardened heart (Exodus 7:1-5) shed light on this difficult passage?

_____

_____

_____

17. Why does Moses remind the people of what they had seen (3:21)?

_____

_____

_____

18. Why did Moses plead with God to let him enter the Promised Land?

_____

_____

_____

19. How did God encourage Moses, even as He refused his request?

_____

_____

_____

Apply what you have learned. Do you face obstacles in your life that are as large or as frightening as the Canaanites appeared to the Israelites? How will you obediently *"take possession of the land"* (1:8) that God has given you? Focus on His promise in 3:22 as you experience difficult situations and people in your life. Be confident in His care and protection as you see His promises unfold in your life.

Israel, God's People
Deuteronomy 1–3

Moses, Israel's faithful leader, wrote almost all of Deuteronomy. He repeatedly emphasized that the bond between God and Israel rested on *God's* faithfulness but would be fully experienced only when Israel obeyed.

God's Command

Moses reminds the Israelites that God wants them to *"take possession of the land"* He has promised them (1:8). Despite their apprehension, obedience is essential. Forty years before, God's people had crossed the desert to the Canaan border in 11 days—but they complained, wept, and rebelled as they went (Numbers 10–12).

A Crisis and Its Consequences

Moses recounts that he had agreed with the leaders' request to send 12 men to spy out the land and strategize for its conquest. Ten men reported insurmountable obstacles. Only Caleb and Joshua disagreed. They recommended taking the land, but the people would not listen. Influenced by the 10 spies who gave the negative report, the Israelites grumbled and rebelled.

The people and Moses looked at the same situation, but through different lenses. Moses examined with faith—*"See, the Lord your God has set the land before you"* (1:21). But the doubting people concluded that God hated them and had brought them out of Egypt only to be destroyed. So God pronounced judgment: No one from *"this evil generation"* would enter Canaan (1:35). Still, God rewarded Caleb and Joshua for their faith. He exempted Caleb and his family from judgment and named Joshua as the one to lead Israel into the land (1:38). As a consequence of Moses' previous disobedience, God denied Moses entrance into the Promised Land (1:37).

> **Think about** how we don't especially like to hear about our failures or the failures of our forefathers. We'd rather focus on our past achievements. But God loves us so much that He will not tolerate faithlessness. He uses our failures to demonstrate His grace toward us and teach us to depend on Him. As our loving Father, He helps us become the people He created us to be.

Wilderness Years

After their refusal to enter Canaan, God had commanded the Israelites to turn again to the north. They obediently bypassed Edom and came to Moab (Numbers 20:14-21). God desired that Israel respect the Moabites and Ammonites as they had the Edomites. But Sihon, the king of the Amorites, provoked conflict with the Israelites as they attempted to cross his land peaceably.

> **Think about** how God desired that the Israelites reflect His character so that the nations around them could come to know Him. God's people, wherever we are, must show the people around us the way to God. As Israel did, we may have to "go out of our way" to demonstrate honor and respect for the people God loves!

Conquest and Possession of the Promised Land

Moses sent messengers to King Sihon requesting peace and permission for the Israelites to pass through his land to the border (2:26-30). Moses assured King Sihon that the Israelites would stay on the main highway. Their purchase of food and water along the way would benefit the Amorites financially. Their only goal was to cross the Jordan River to occupy the land God had promised them as their possession.

Sihon, however, refused to allow passage (2:30). So God enabled them to defeat him and capture his cities. Then King Og of Bashan attacked them with "*all his people*" (3:1), and again God gave Israel victory in battle.

Pay attention to two implicit truths in Deuteronomy. The first is cultural, the second theological. First, Deuteronomy 2:32-35 describes warfare tactics that may offend most modern readers. The Israelites completely destroyed property and people. Completely destroy, from the Hebrew *herem*, indicates something being *utterly devoted to God*. In ancient Near Eastern nations, the philosophy of war sometimes came down to a choice—destroy the other nation completely or be completely destroyed. Israel knew that survival required complete destruction of the enemy: "*When the Lord your God gives them over to you, and you defeat them, then you must devote them to complete destruction*" (7:2). Fortunately, Israel's wars usually did not go to this extreme, but required only a show of power against nations threatening them with annihilation or enslavement.

Deuteronomy also illustrates a second truth—God has chosen to work within human history. To do this He accepts certain human methods and limitations as He works His purposes. Note that God fights for Israel—Israel doesn't fight for God!

The Israelites had conquered 60 Amorite cities throughout this fertile area. "*All these were cities fortified with high walls, gates, and bars,*" and were the ones that the 10 Hebrew spies, 38 years earlier, had represented as insurmountable obstacles. Moses reminds Israel of what he had told Joshua, "*Your eyes have seen all that the Lord your God has done to these two kings*" (3:21).

With a deep longing in his heart, Moses appeals to God. "*Please let me go over and see the good land beyond the Jordan, that good hill country and Lebanon.*" Deuteronomy 3:23-25 exposes two important points:

1. There is a true depth of love and freedom between God and His servant Moses; Moses is relaxed and honest in his prayer.

2. It is Moses' nature to persist. It is this characteristic that enabled him to lead these oft-complaining people.

On a previous occasion, Moses had asked God to relent from His decision to destroy His people—and God heard Moses and agreed! (See Exodus 32:12-14; Deuteronomy 9:13-14.) This time, however, God refuses Moses' request. Still, God does not ignore Moses' deep longing. "*Go up to the top of* [Mount] *Pisgah and lift your eyes ... and look at it with your own eyes*" (2:27). Moses then turns to the task of preparing Joshua.

Personalize this lesson.

☑ God planned for the Israelites to live in the Promised Land as His people and be a testimony to His glory before all nations. As Christians, our goal is to live in the world for Christ, as a testimony to His glory in the face of indifference. Just as God provided all that Israel needed for her success, He also provides for our needs, too. *"His divine power has granted to us all things that pertain to life and godliness, ... He has granted to us His precious and very great promises, so that through them you may become partakers of the divine nature, having escaped from the corruption that is in the world because of sinful desire"* (2 Peter 1:3-4).

Do you see God working His will throughout Deuteronomy 1–3? Trust God to fight for you just as He fought for the Israelites. We can't always explain why things happen in our lives, but we can always rest in the protection of His precious promises.

God's Mighty Acts and Righteous Law
Deuteronomy 4–5

❖ Deuteronomy 4:1-14—Obeying God

1. *"And now, O Israel, listen"* (4:1). The Hebrew word for *listen* means *to comprehend and actively respond* rather than merely to hear words. How do verses 1-4 tell us to respond?

   _____

   _____

   _____

2. How will non-believers respond when they see believers obey God?

   _____

   _____

   _____

3. How does your walk with God affect the people around you?

   _____

   _____

   _____

❖ Deuteronomy 4:15-31—Idolatry

4. How are idols inferior to God?

   _____

   _____

   _____

5. What is the result of idolatry, according to Psalm 115:4-8 and Hosea 9:10?

_____

_____

_____

6. What contemporary idols are you sometimes tempted to worship?

_____

_____

_____

❖ Deuteronomy 4:32-40—God's Greatness

7. What great things did God do?

_____

_____

_____

8. Which of these acts of God is especially meaningful to you? Why?

_____

_____

_____

_____

_____

❖ Deuteronomy 5:6-21—The Ten Commandments of God

9. Why do you think the commandments are introduced with the words of 5:6?

_____

_____

_____

10. How is God's truth diminished when we misuse His name?

   _____

   _____

11. Why does God insist that the Sabbath be kept holy?

   _____

   _____

12. Read verses 16-21 thoughtfully. How would our world be different if everyone obeyed these commandments?

   _____

   _____

   _____

   _____

   _____

13. Given the beneficial nature of God's laws, why is it sometimes hard for us to obey them?

   _____

   _____

   _____

❖ Deuteronomy 5:22-33—Israel's Response

14. From 5:22-33, what emotions did God's nearness evoke in His people?

   _____

   _____

15. Can you describe a time when you've experienced God's presence? How did His nearness affect your faith?

   _____

   _____

   _____

16. What did God's people intend to do (5:27-29)?

_____

_____

_____

17. From 5:29-33, what did God promise if the people obeyed?

_____

_____

_____

18. According to Judges 2:1-12, what happened to their good intentions before long?

_____

_____

_____

19. What is the warning in this for you?

_____

_____

_____

Apply what you have learned. Think of the principles found in the Ten Commandments (all of which are reinforced in the New Testament) as traffic signals. Is God trying to tell you to "Stop" and reassess your behavior? Is He telling you to "Go," to continue what you're doing now, or to follow your instincts about trying something new? Or are you feeling a "Caution," a hesitancy to proceed? Is God giving you a red light, green light, yellow light? Slow down and read God's Ten Commandments one more time. What area do you sense He would like you to focus on this week? How can you carry through with your good intentions to obey?

God's Mighty Acts and Righteous Law
Deuteronomy 4–5

As the Israelites stood poised at the border of the Promised Land, Moses spoke to them. He reminded them of God's love and mighty power at the time of the Exodus. They had not become the people of God *through* the Exodus—they were *already* His chosen people. At Horeb (Mount Sinai) they had seen the signs of His Presence and heard Him speak. God had given them the Ten Commandments so they could live before other nations as "*a wise and understanding people.*"

Obeying God

"*And now, O Israel, listen*"—Moses wants the people's full attention as he continues his first address prior to crossing the Jordan River. He emphasizes that blessing and joy follow obedience, while discipline and sorrow often result from disobedience.

Idolatry

Addressing especially the older Israelites before him, Moses warns them to never forget what "*your eyes have seen* [when] ... *you stood before the Lord your God at Horeb*" (4:9-14). As young adults, they had "seen" God in the miracles of the Exodus, the sound and light that engulfed the mountain of Horeb, and the supernatural daily provisions for 40 years of wilderness wandering. Moses warns them not to represent their God with man-made images. Nor should they worship the sun, the moon, the stars, or any created thing. If they step away from God's covenant, they step into God's judgment—"*a consuming fire*" (4:24).

God's Greatness

These beautiful verses elaborate on God's compassion and faithfulness in Israel's history. Moses focuses on God's nature. Had "*such a great thing as this ... ever happened or* [been] *heard of?"* (4:32). Viewing the panorama of human history, no other nation has had an experience to match Israel's Exodus.

The Ten Commandments

Moses opens with a summary of historical events (4:44-49); he then repeats the same Law given at Mount Horeb as a renewal of the covenant. Israel is to hear in order to learn and follow God's laws. At Horeb, God's awesome manifestation terrified the Israelites. So God appointed Moses as His mediator with them. God asserts His authority over Israel: *"I am the LORD your God, who brought you out of the land of Egypt, out of the house of slavery"* (5:6). God redeemed Israel, delivered His people from slavery, and led them to Horeb. The first four commandments frame the relationship between God and His people. The last six deal specifically with person-to-person relationships. The former is essential to the latter.

- Although the first commandment, *"You shall have no other gods before Me"* (5:7), is cast in a negative form, it has positive implications. Be faithful to God who has always provided for Israel.

- The second commandment forbids representing God in any physical shape or form.

- *"You shall not take the name of the LORD your God in vain"* (5:11) prohibits using God's name in an attempt to control His power for personal gain. Canaanites commonly uttered magical incantations in the power of a god's name. The one true God was above such human manipulation: *"For the LORD will not hold him guiltless who takes His name in vain"* (5:11).

Think about how, in Moses' day, using anyone's name implied a certain power over that person; to use God's name to gain one's own ends was supremely sacrilegious. We think of the third commandment mainly as forbidding the use of God's name as a swear word. But there are different ways to misuse His name—all of which we want to avoid because His name is holy!

- The fourth commandment is: "*Observe the Sabbath day, to keep it holy*" (5:12). While enslaved in Egypt, they likely worked continuously without a day of rest. As a newly formed nation of God's people, they are to follow His example established at Creation: six days of work and one of *shabat, rest.*

- The fifth commandment— "*honor your father and your mother*" (5:16). All Israel is charged to respect those who parent on earth.

- "*You shall not murder*" (5:17) deals specifically with murder. It does not eliminate the taking of life in war (Deuteronomy 20–21) nor eliminate the possibility of capital punishment (Deuteronomy 17:2-7; 19:12). Here, God forbids *murder (premeditated killing)*.

- "*You shall not commit adultery*" (5:18) prohibits sexual relationships between two persons, one or both of whom are married to another. Unfaithfulness to a marriage partner also implies unfaithfulness to God.

- "*You shall not steal*" (5:19). Certainly this command prohibits simple theft (Exodus 22:1-13), but the primary interpretation was probably to guard against the worst kind of theft—kidnapping in order to enslave.

- "*You shall not bear false witness against your neighbor*" (5:20) forbids lying and deception, leading to slander and defamation of another person's character.

- The 10th commandment, "*You shall not covet*" (5:21), addresses motivation rather than deed. Commandments six through nine prohibit wrong acts toward neighbors; commandment 10 penetrates to the very core of all previous commandments.

Moses concludes with a warning for Israel to be careful to walk in the way of the Lord. This is their responsibility as God's covenant people.

Personalize this lesson.

☑ God clearly promised the Israelites that if they kept His decrees, all would go well with them and their children in the land. The Ten Commandments were meant for their good—and for ours. God is always acting on behalf of His people, so they might respond to His love. These commands are essentially liberating. The first—to have no other gods before the one God—is the foundation on which the other nine stand. When God is first in our lives, we will set up no false gods, and we will seek to honor God in all we do.

Take some time to let God talk to you about the place He has in your life. Is He truly first? Then thank Him and praise Him! Are there things that rival for first place—the need for status, financial security, control, affirmation, etc.? Talk to Him about these. Ask Him to help your trust in Him to be all you need—to truly be your God—and let Him have first place in your heart.

To Love and Obey
Deuteronomy 6–7

Memorize God's Word: Deuteronomy 5:33.

❖ Deuteronomy 6:1-6—The Greatest Command

1. Why should we obey God's commands?

   _____

   _____

   _____

2. Do you think God's commands are positive or negative? Why?

   _____

   _____

   _____

   _____

   _____

3. Read Matthew 22:34-40 with Deuteronomy 6:4-6. How do you explain Jesus' statement that this is the most important commandment?

   _____

   _____

   _____

   _____

   _____

❖ Deuteronomy 6:7-25—God's Warnings

4. What does Moses warn the Israelites not to do (6:10-12)?

    _____

    _____

5. How does that warning apply to us today?

    _____

    _____

6. What are the benefits of *fearing* God?

    _____

    _____

7. In Deuteronomy 6:14-17, what three things does God require of
    His people?

    _____

    _____

    _____

8. In 6:20-25, Moses told parents to recount certain things to their
    children. What do you think parents today should be passing
    along to their children and grandchildren?

    _____

    _____

    _____

❖ Deuteronomy 7:1-11—The Difficult Command
Note: Please limit your response to the specific questions asked. The
next lesson will consider this difficult subject in more detail.

9. How do you think laws of war today differ from those listed in
    7:1-6?

    _____

    _____

    _____

10. What reasons did Moses give implicitly or explicitly for such severe demands?

_____

_____

_____

11. What are God's reasons for favoring the Israelites?

_____

_____

_____

12. Read 1 Peter 2:9-10. How do you feel about being one of God's beloved children?

_____

_____

_____

❖ Deuteronomy 7:12-26—The Covenant Between God and Man

13. What prevents the Israelites from trusting God?

_____

_____

_____

14. How does God reassure them?

_____

_____

_____

15. How does God reassure you in times of doubt and fear?

_____

_____

_____

16. In verses 12-16, what did Israel have to do in order to experience the benefits of God's love?

_____

_____

_____

17. What were the benefits?

_____

_____

_____

18. Read John 14:15-21. What is the relationship between obedience and love?

_____

_____

_____

Apply what you have learned. Read and reread the *Shema* (Deuteronomy 6:4-9). What does it mean to you to love God with "*all your heart ... soul ... and might*"? Is there anything that keeps you from enthusiastically loving Him? What do you need to do to love Him in the way He wants you to love?

Intentionally express your love for God this week with all of your heart, soul, and might. Memorize 6:5 or teach it to a child. Make God part of everyday conversations with people around you. Commit to obeying Him wholeheartedly in response to His love for you so that it will "*go well with you*" (6:3).

To Love and Obey
Deuteronomy 6–7

Obedience continues to permeate Moses' message in this passage. Israel must now settle an occupied territory, so Moses urges God's people to remember and obey His commandments—*"that it may go well with you"* (6:3). God promised Israel this land, but Israel must obey Him to receive His blessings.

The Greatest Command

Known in Jewish tradition as the *Shema* (Hebrew for *hear*), 6:4-9 expresses the central truth of Israel's religion. The basic assertion, *"The LORD our God, the LORD is one,"* distinguished Israel from her polytheistic environment. Israel was to acknowledge, love, and worship Yahweh alone. Jesus later identified the *Shema* as the *"great and first commandment"* (Matthew 22:34-38).

God's covenant with Israel is built on love, initiated by God. The Lord brought them out of slavery and sustained them in the wilderness because He loved them. In return, Moses reminds them, *"You shall love the LORD your God with all your heart and with all your soul and with all your might"* (6:5). Three small words—heart, soul, and might—show how Israel should respond in a big way to God's great love and provision. God's total devotion to His people clearly demands their total devotion in return.

Moses exhorts Israel to keep God's words in their hearts. But they shouldn't stop there. They need to *"teach* [God's commands] *diligently to your children, and ... talk of them when you sit in your house, and when you walk by the way, and when you lie down, and when you rise"* (6:7). Moses even directs them to write God's commandments on their hands, doorposts, and gates as a visible reminder of God's covenant of love with them.

God's Warnings

Moses poetically portrays the Promised Land's bounty in 6:10-11. Then he warns, "*Take care lest you forget the LORD, who brought you out of the land of Egypt*" (6:12). The land's very goodness could lull them into disastrous pride. Moses reminds them, "*It is the LORD your God you shall fear. Him you shall serve*" (6:13). Instead of testing God by expecting Him to meet their own conditions, the Israelites are to serve Him. Successfully taking the land depends on their obedience.

The Difficult Command

Israel's only hope for survival in the Promised Land is careful obedience. After conquering the land and its occupants, Israel "*must devote them to complete destruction*" (7:2). God is judging Canaan, and He is blessing Israel. Do you realize why God did not immediately give Abraham the land he was promised? God's mercy allowed the Canaanites time to turn from their wickedness. Now, centuries later, Canaanite religious practices (including child sacrifice, idol worship, religious prostitution, and sexual abuses) are rampant. God knows that Israel's fragile faith cannot survive in Canaan's harsh, idolatrous climate. To preserve His people, God gives Israel this difficult command.

Think about how difficult it is not to be influenced by ungodly actions that surround us. In a world where seemingly anything goes, we must keep our hearts turned toward God. Remember, our obedience brings God's blessings.

"*Fear the LORD your God ... [keep] all ... His commandments ...all the days of your life ... that your days may be long ... that it may go well with you ... as the LORD, the God of your fathers, has promised you*" (6:2-3). Claim His promises by trusting in His mercy and obeying His commands.

Note that Scripture never uses the term *Holy War*. The Bible does not glorify or glamorize war. War is simply one of many evidences of sin in our world. And God uses human means to bring about His purposes. In Deuteronomy 7, God tells Israel how to treat the people He has enabled them to conquer. Clearly, Israel's task is to rid their land of all that threatens their existence as God's people.

God must protect Israel from destruction and spiritual contamination because His eternal purpose is to bless the world with a Savior, Jesus Christ, through Israel. "*The LORD your God has chosen you ... out of all the peoples who are on the face of the earth*" (7:6).

Covenant Between God and Man

Why did God choose Israel? Moses states simply that the Israelites were God's "*treasured possession*" (7:6) and that "*the LORD loves you*" (7:8). The reason for God's special love and choice of Israel remains a mystery. But there is no mystery behind the importance of Israel's obedience. Israel's future depends on it: "*Because you listen to these rules and keep and do them, the LORD your God will keep with you the covenant and the steadfast love that He swore to your fathers*" (7:12).

The Israelites are nomads who will now become first-time landowners. Rookies in crop production, they must depend on God for prosperity—unlike the Canaanites who trusted in their idols for good harvests. God remembered how easily Israel had previously ignored His command to refrain from idol worship despite His constant, visible presence in the pillars of cloud and fire (Exodus 14:19-20). Now, Israel must learn to live by obedience and faith alone.

God's love and blessing extended to all spheres of life. Israel's population would increase as God had promised Abraham. Their crops of grain, wine, and oil would be abundant. Herds of cattle and flocks of lambs would increase.

Moses also alerts the Israelites to the dangers ahead. When they encounter the enemy, they should not succumb to terror or pity, because God will deliver the enemy into their hands. Settlement will take time, as God will drive out the nations "*little by little*" (7:22). This gradual takeover actually protects Israel. If the enemy fled and suddenly vacated large tracts of land, wild animals would multiply and cultivated areas would revert to weeds. "*Little by little*," Israel will move into the Promised Land under God's protective care.

Personalize this lesson.

✓ We are not told why God loved the Israelites, only that He did. Similarly, God loves us because He is love, not necessarily because the object of His love is lovable. He loves freely and, in fact, chooses to love those whom people often reject. He does not love us more when we are good or less when we have sinned. And as His love is, so His mercy is everlasting. No matter how grievously the Israelites sinned against God, He did not abandon them. God loves freely, everlastingly, patiently, compassionately. His faithfulness does not fluctuate.

Is your love for God as constant as His is for you? Or does it fluctuate, depending on how you feel, how life is going for you, if He's answered your prayers, and so on? Ask God to help you be as faithful in your love for Him as He is in His love for you. Then pay attention to opportunities to express your love to Him when things are going well for you and when they are not.

Israel Needs to Choose
Deuteronomy 8–11

❖ Deuteronomy 8:1–9:6—Remember, Do Not Forget

1. Do you think the Promised Land is a greater test for Israel than the wilderness? Why or why not?

_____

_____

_____

2. What aspects of modern life do you think are the greatest test to people who seek to walk with God?

_____

_____

_____

3. In this passage, how did God demonstrate His faithfulness to Israel?

_____

_____

_____

4. What do you learn about God and how He relates to people?

_____

_____

_____

_____

5. Read Exodus 23:31-33 with Deuteronomy 9:1-6. Why is it necessary to remove the Canaanites completely?

❖ Deuteronomy 9:7-24—Israel's Memory

6. Read and compare 9:7-14, 23-24 and 5:26-29. How would you describe the Israelites' usual behavior?

---

7. How would you describe their concept of themselves?

---

8. How does this understanding add meaning to 9:4-6?

❖ Deuteronomy 9:25–10:11—Moses Prays

9. Can you find phrases that suggest the intensity and personal nature of Moses' intercessory prayer in verses 25-29?

---

10. What is the heart of the prayer?

---

11. How does God respond to Moses' prayer? Why?

_____

_____

_____

❖ Deuteronomy 10:12-22—Requirements and Rewards

12. Refer to at least one of these cross-references to explain these phrases in verse 12.

   a. *"Fear the LORD your God"*: Leviticus 19:13-18; Ecclesiastes 12:13-14; 1 Peter 2:16-17.

   _____

   _____

   b. *"Walk in all His ways"*: Genesis 17:1; Jeremiah 7:23; Galatians 5:16.

   _____

   _____

   c. *"Love Him"*: Deuteronomy 30:20; Psalm 18:1-3; John 14:21-24; 1 John 5:3.

   _____

   _____

❖ Deuteronomy 11—Obeying God

13. According to this passage, what must Israel do to obey God?

   _____

   _____

   _____

14. What reasons are stated for obedience?

   _____

   _____

   _____

15. Obedience to God is a key theme in Deuteronomy and has been emphasized since chapter 5. According to 11:22-25, what will be the reward for obedience?

   _____

   _____

   _____

16. What contrasting terms does Moses use (11:26-32) to emphasize the results of their choices?

   _____

   _____

   _____

17. Why do you think God commands them to stand on two mountains inside Canaan rather than on the other side of the Jordan to "*set*" or proclaim those terms (11:29)?

   _____

   _____

   _____

Apply what you have learned. Moses reminded the Israelites that bread is not the only thing necessary for life—God's Word is (8:3). And Jesus reiterated that truth when He told Satan, "*Man shall not live by bread alone, but by every word that comes from the mouth of God*" (Matthew 4:4). What are some of the words from God that bring life to you? Start a list and try to add at least one new one to your list each day.

Israel Needs to Choose
Deuteronomy 8–11

In his message to Israel, Moses emphasizes the covenant that God established with them at Horeb. Now Moses continues to stress the importance of maintaining this relationship with God. He reminds the Israelites of tragic past experiences involving rebellion toward God.

Remember—Do Not Forget

To emphasize the call to obedience, Moses uses two contrasting themes: "remember/forget" and "wilderness/Promised Land." Moses had seen one generation die in the wilderness because of rebellion and sin. So he urges the Israelites to *"remember"* the wilderness and God's presence there. The miraculous supply of manna and water demonstrated their absolute dependence on Him. But Israel has weaknesses: (1) They lack humility. Their attitude about the great Exodus has already shifted from gratitude to pride. (2) They must distinguish between physical and spiritual food—to learn that God is the ultimate resource for both. God and His Word were their basic source of life. When Jesus was tempted in the wilderness, He used this very text as an unchanging principle of dependence on God and His Word.

Moses' crucial advice to not *"forget the Lord your God"* (8:11) will help them avoid complacency that may result from the peace they will experience in the Promised Land. To guard against pride, they must remember God's gracious acts. Moses specifically mentions four: (1) God brought them out of slavery; (2) God led them through the wilderness; (3) God provided water in the desert; (4) God gave them manna to eat. They were not self-sufficient—they were indebted to God. So they were not free to do as they pleased when they crossed the Jordan River. The Israelites must guard against presuming that they have achieved their new-found security and peace through their own actions alone.

Think about how the 40 years Israel spent in the desert was a time of discipline. They were tempted to doubt God's goodness when things got tough, and they often grumbled. Now they face prosperity with all its temptations. No situation in life is without its dangers to faith. Adversity tempts us to forget God's goodness. Prosperity, too, may tempt us to forget Him. Remembering God and His goodness—at all times, under all conditions—protects us and our faith.

Israel's Failure, God's Mercy, and Grace

The powerful nations Israel will face beyond the Jordan are secure in fortified cities. God would give Israel victory, but they are required to fight the battles. God is expelling these wicked nations to honor His covenant with Abraham, Isaac, and Jacob. God will pave the way for Israel to possess Canaan, fulfilling His promise made centuries earlier and confirming His covenant with His people.

Despite God's continued grace, Israel's stubborn attitude persists. Moses reminds them that they had *"provoked the LORD to wrath, and the LORD was so angry with you that He was ready to destroy you"* (9:8). Even while Moses met with God on Mount Horeb, the people had *"turned aside quickly"* (9:12). Because of their sin, God had threatened to destroy the Israelites and blot out their name. As he descended the mountain from the awesome glory of God's presence, Moses had seen the *"golden calf"* (9:16). Moses reiterates how—shocked by the people's flagrant disregard of both the first and second commandments—he broke the stone tablets of the covenant and fervently interceded on their behalf.

Moses Prays

Moses reminds the people of his appeals to God's covenant faithfulness, seeking forgiveness on Israel's behalf despite their well-deserved discipline. Moses had pleaded with God to show His undeserved love to the Israelites and vindicate His own honor, *"for they are Your people and Your heritage"* (9:29).

God had responded to Moses' request with mercy, instructing him to prepare new tablets and a wooden ark to hold them. God engraved this treaty Himself as a testimony to His *faithfulness* in the face of their *faithlessness*. In answer to Moses' humble prayer, God had spared His people from the consequences of their idolatry.

Think about how the obstinate, rebellious Israelites often severely tested Moses' patience, but he did not give up. Moses persevered in intercessory prayer rather than agree when God threatened to destroy this "*stubborn people*" (9:13). God even hinted that He was tired of hearing Moses' petitions. But Moses prayed on.

Persistent, persevering, patient prayer. We often face times when it seems God doesn't hear our prayers, but discouragement is deadly in our prayer lives. Follow Moses' lead and continue to pray for His will as you intercede for others as well as pray for yourself. "*The prayer of a righteous person has great power as it is working*" (James 5:16).

Moses reminds them that God loved their forefathers and "*chose their offspring ... you above all peoples*" (10:15). Moses realizes Israel's heart must soften and change in order to respond to God's command. He pleads, "*Circumcise ... your heart, and be no longer stubborn*" (10:16).

Because of His character, God will not accept legalistic obedience to His commandments as a substitute for wholehearted commitment in love. Moses urges them to acknowledge that God has fulfilled His promise to make them "*as numerous as the stars of heaven*" (10:22), and He has delivered them to the border of the Promised Land. If the people love God, God's love will be freely demonstrated. If they turn to other gods, however, God's anger will result.

Choose God

Moses urges the Israelites to make right choices because God has chosen to relate lovingly with His people. Love cannot be forced; it must be chosen. God has given the Israelites the freedom to choose other gods or Him.

Personalize this lesson.

✓ God presents good choices to us, but He does not compel decision. Moses pointed out that choices, inevitably, have consequences. Obedience to God brings blessing, and disobedience brings disaster.

We may not have been called to settle the Promised Land, but we are directed *"to walk in a manner worthy of the calling to which you have been called"* (Ephesians 4:1). Choose to fear God, to walk in all His ways, to love and serve Him as you follow His commands. Persistently ask God to soften your heart to enable you to comply with His will—because His blessings follow your obedience.

How to Worship God
Deuteronomy 12, 13, & 26

Memorize God's Word: Deuteronomy 11:18-19.

❖ Deuteronomy 12—Be God's People

1. What are God's instructions about Canaanite worship (12:1-4)?

   _____

   _____

   _____

   _____

2. Read 1 Kings 11:1-11. How does Solomon's story show the appropriateness of God's instructions?

   _____

   _____

   _____

   _____

   _____

   _____

3. What does Deuteronomy 12:8 imply about Israel at that time?

   _____

   _____

   _____

❖ Deuteronomy 12—How to Worship

4. Refer to 12:5-32, and list at least five instructions about worship. For each, suggest why God required it.

Instruction	Reason
1)	
2)	
3)	
4)	
5)	

5. How could believers apply one or more of these instructions today?

_____

_____

_____

❖ Deuteronomy 13—Dangers of Idolatry

6. What do you learn from 13:1-5 about our individual responsibility concerning religious leaders and God?

_____

_____

_____

7. How do power, signs, and wonders affect people?

_____

_____

_____

8. Why do you think discernment is needed when signs and wonders are demonstrated?

_____

_____

_____

9. Who are the three groups mentioned in this passage who might mislead believers' faith?

_____

_____

10. How can these groups continue to apply pressure and confuse believers today?

_____

_____

_____

11. In light of chapter 13 as a whole, why are verses 3-4 significant?

_____

_____

_____

❖ Deuteronomy 26—Remember and Rejoice

12. Read Deuteronomy 26:2-11. What do you consider the most important information in this passage, and why?

_____

_____

_____

13. Why is remembering the past an important part of worship?

_____

_____

_____

❖ Deuteronomy 26—Worship and Celebration

14. According to 26:10-11, what should characterize Israel's worship?

15. Read Deuteronomy 26:12-15. What is the command in verse 12, and what is its purpose?

16. In one word, summarize the Israelites' behavior in verses 13-15.

17. In one word, what is the expected result?

Apply what you have learned. *Firstfruits* are agricultural products that ripen earliest and represent the coming harvest. The people offered firstfruits to God in remembrance of His provision. The offering was a part of proper worship for Israel. But, as is always the case in proper worship, the offering also benefited the community. Those who were without land, or without a way to produce their own food, were to eat this offering.

Although it's essential to "look up" to God, we should also "look out" for fellow worshipers. When we truly worship God, we mature into believers truly committed to each other in Him. We may not have actual fruit that we've harvested from our gardens to give to God, but we do have God-given time, talents, and treasures. Think about the gifts God has showered on you. What is one *"firstfruits"* offering you can give to Him this week?

How to Worship God
Deuteronomy 12, 13, & 26

Forty years after the Exodus, Moses reminds the people that they disobediently refused to conquer the Promised Land despite being God's *"treasured possession"* (7:6). Israel is God's chosen nation, and He requires His people to love, serve, and obey Him exclusively and wholeheartedly. Obedience remains Moses' theme throughout these chapters.

No Idols

Moses directs the people to destroy the Canaanite altars and shrines as he cautions them to follow God's laws. The Canaanites believed that their god Baal owned and inhabited the highest places in the land, and they marked their worship sites with stones, pillars, poles, or trees. They were convinced that they were totally dependent on their pagan gods for a good harvest.

God abhorred this type of worship. Now that Israel was an agricultural nation, they were susceptible to their pagan neighbors' worship practices. God required complete destruction of the pagan high places to remove temptations for the Israelites. God wanted to protect their purity, so He commanded, *"You shall not worship the LORD your God in that way"* (12:4).

Think about how *syncretism*, a term which means *to combine two opposite principles or philosophies* (in this case, gods), was common in the Israelites' time. God reminded His people that He was the only God. Exposed to many false gods in Egypt, the Israelites were once again surrounded by idolatrous people. So Moses directed them to destroy all the high places and cleanse the land.

Think about the idols we tend to worship today. God warns
that we must not mix idolatry with Christianity. Just as the
Israelites needed to stay true to God, we need to resist this
world's values and attitudes and remain faithful to Him, too.
Studying God's Word is a wonderful way to discern what we
need to do to remain true to Him.

How to Worship

Even though there are many pagan worship areas scattered conveniently
throughout the Promised Land, God protects His people by limiting
their choices. Moses instructs them to worship God only in *"the place
that the* LORD *your God will choose"* (12:5). When the people come
to God's designated place to worship, Moses reminds them to *"bring
your burnt offerings and your sacrifices, your tithes … and the firstborn
of your herd and of your flock"* (12:6). The burnt offering—which was
completely consumed—represented the people's total commitment to
God-pleasing lives. Sacrifices also represented salvation, thanksgiving,
praise, or a vow to God. Tithes (a 10th) were measured out in grains, oils,
wines, and firstborn animals. When the people have been in the land
long enough to harvest grains and grapes, their offerings will remind
them that their prosperity is God's blessing.

Moses then encourages God's people to worship joyfully: *"Rejoice before
the* LORD *your God in all that you undertake"* (12:18). God would provide
Israel's harvests and herds, and He simply desired that His people respond
with joy. Moses reminds them that God desires His people to worship
in community and welcome outsiders. Parents will acknowledge God's
goodness with their children, and servants will join in the feasting and
celebration (12:7, 18-19).

Dangers of Idolatry

Unlike the surrounding nations, Israel has no pantheon of gods
demanding appeasement and violent ritual offerings. Her God is not
"in nature," but above nature as its Creator and Sustainer. He is not
represented by man-made images. Instead, Israel's God loves His people,
desires their well-being, and teaches them to rejoice in worship.

But Moses knows that the Israelites will struggle with idolatrous
influences from the pagan cultures bordering their new land. He focuses

on God's consequences for leaders who promote idolatry. Deliberately undermining allegiance to God is a dangerous crime in Israel. Moses gravely warns of three groups of people who might lead Israel to idolatry: religious leaders, family and friends, or an entire, unbelieving city. Idolatry has no place among God's people. The penalty in each case will be capital punishment. The nature of the crime—deliberately influencing people to renounce their loyalty to God—is the reason for the punishment's severity. Faithfulness to God is absolutely essential for Israel's continued existence. Although such punishment is difficult to understand, it is necessary for the survival of God's people.

Worship and Celebration

For 40 years, the Israelites have been nomads; before that, they were oppressed slaves in Egypt. But in Canaan they will live in towns and villages, own property, raise crops, and graze cattle, goats, and sheep. Israelites will reflect their gratefulness to God with offerings of these crops and animals. The Israelites, for the first time, will observe two ceremonies *"when you come into the land that the* LORD *your God is giving you"* (26:1). They will offer firstfruits of the ground and, later, they will offer the triennial tithe.

First, God's people will offer *firstfruits* (the grains or fruit that ripen first) and testify to God's faithfulness. They will remember God's deliverance, retelling the stories of how He exercised His power to rescue them from slavery in Egypt and bring them into the land He promised them (26:5). In contrast to the Canaanites—who credit their inanimate idols for providing fruitful crops and good soil—the Israelites' celebration will demonstrate that they recognize the one true God as the Giver of their abundant harvests. They will affirm that *Yahweh* alone has graced the land with fruitfulness as they *"rejoice in all the good that the* LORD *... has given"* (26:11). Again, Moses emphasizes sharing with outsiders by including *"the sojourner who is among you"* in the festivities.

Two years later, a second ceremony will take place in their communities. God's people will bring tithes to distribute to the Levites, the aliens, the fatherless, and the widows. They will declare before God that they have fulfilled the tithe-sharing requirement, blessing less fortunate people.

Moses concludes by asking for renewed allegiance to God's covenant. Then, the people declare their intention to keep His commandments and walk in His ways—to receive His blessings.

Personalize this lesson.

☑ In worship we revere and honor God, who alone deserves it. Worship is both an attitude of heart and mind and also the actions by which we express that attitude. Although, as believers, our worship ceremonies may differ, worship's essential purpose is unchanged. When we worship, we submit our lives to Him and seek to understand more about Him and His will for our lives. How is your heart responding to God's call of worship? To sing? Express words of praise? Kneel before Him in silence? Give an offering of gratitude? Make a commitment to walk more closely with Him? Consider one or two ways you might more intentionally offer God the worship He deserves—and then follow through during the next week.

Celebrating God's Grace
Deuteronomy 16:1-17

❖ **Deuteronomy 16:1-8—Passover and the Feast of Unleavened Bread**

1. Read Exodus 12:1-14. How does the place of the original Passover described in Exodus differ from the place of this feast mentioned in Deuteronomy?

    _____

    _____

    _____

    _____

    _____

2. What do you think is the significance of this change?

    _____

    _____

    _____

3. Leaven (often translated *yeast*) is used in the Feast of Weeks (Leviticus 23:17), yet prohibited in the Feast of Unleavened Bread (Deuteronomy 16:3). Why?

    _____

    _____

    _____

    _____

    _____

4. Besides the practical purpose unleavened bread served in the first Passover celebration, what spiritual meaning might it suggest? (See Matthew 13:33, 16:6, 12; 1 Corinthians 5:1-2, 6-8; Galatians 5:7-10.)

_____

_____

_____

❖ Deuteronomy 16:9-12—The Feast of Weeks

5. Who participates in this feast, and what are they instructed to do?

_____

_____

_____

6. Israel must worship *"at the place that the LORD will choose"* (16:15). According to the book of Joshua, the Israelites had worshiped at several different places soon after entering the land. What is the principle behind the command repeated in Deuteronomy 16:2, 11, and 15?

_____

_____

_____

7. Read Acts 2:1-21, where the Feast of Weeks is called by its Greek name, the Feast of Pentecost. How did onlookers interpret the Christians' joy?

_____

_____

_____

8. What does Peter say is the reason for the Christians' behavior?

_____

_____

_____

❖ Deuteronomy 16:13-17—The Feast of Booths

9. What words indicate the celebratory tone?

_____

_____

_____

_____

10. Do you think these words apply to how you practice your faith? Why or why not?

_____

_____

_____

_____

_____

11. What do you learn about stewardship in this passage?

_____

_____

_____

12. What do you learn about stewardship in 2 Corinthians 9:6-8?

_____

_____

_____

13. Deuteronomy 16:17 tells us that during the Feast of Booths, *"Every man shall give as he is able, according to the blessing of the* LORD *your God."* Read John 7:1-16. How does Jesus give as He is able?

_____

_____

_____

_____

14. In the chart below, record three traditional Christian
    observances that you think are important to the church. Next to
    each, write your thoughts about the appropriate tone for each.

Observances	Appropriate Tone

Apply what you have learned. God
commands His people to remember and celebrate
the anniversaries of His significant saving acts.
Throughout the year, as you celebrate what God has done
for you, think about how you can pour out energy, effort,
and emotion to Him for His faithfulness. Are you joyful
as you remember how God cares and provides for you—
spiritually and physically? Think of new ways to focus on
Him as you rejoice in His goodness. For example, could you
celebrate your spiritual birthday or the spiritual birthdays
of your family members in a significant way? Is there a life-
changing answer to prayer that you could commemorate
with a "thank offering"? Perhaps an Advent wreath or
calendar would help you celebrate Christ's birth in a more
meaningful and joyful way. Be creative as you seek to honor
Him in new ways throughout your lifetime.

Celebrating God's Grace
Deuteronomy 16:1-17

"Remember, do not forget" continues to be Moses' theme as he emphasizes Israel's relationship with God. Israel's men gather in one central worship place to commemorate God's unfailing faithfulness. The Passover (the Feast of Unleavened Bread), the Feast of Weeks, and the Feast of Booths are the three most important feasts that Israel celebrates; they separate Israel from all the neighboring Canaanites and remind them that they are God's people. While Canaanites attempted to appease their gods at their feasts, Israel's joyous gatherings honored the one true God.

With the exception of Passover, these feasts began only after the Israelites had lived in the land long enough to plant and harvest crops. All three celebrations point to God's covenant renewal with His people: "*I am making a covenant. Before all your people I will do marvels ... all the people ... shall see the work of the Lord, for it is an awesome thing that I will do with you*" (Exodus 34:10).

The Passover and the Feast of Unleavened Bread

The Israelites observed the first Passover on their departure from Egypt, probably in March–April. They observed the second Passover one year later, before their departure from Mount Horeb. They would not celebrate the Passover again until they were in the Promised Land. Moses preaches about that first Passover in Deuteronomy 16.

For the Passover observance, the Israelites killed a young sheep or goat as a sacrificial offering. Families celebrated the first Passover in their homes in Egypt, after applying blood to their doorframes to provide protection from divine judgment. In Canaan, Israel celebrated the Passover as a pilgrimage feast traveling to the Lord's sanctuary to remember their deliverance and the Exodus.

Israel celebrated the Feast of Unleavened Bread in conjunction with the Passover sacrifice. This seven-day feast started on the morning after the Passover celebration. All Israel ate unleavened bread, with the absence of yeast perhaps symbolizing the purity required for God's people. Also, they could bake unleavened bread quickly, so it may have been their staple diet while in Egypt. Moses describes this food as *"the bread of affliction— for you came out of the land of Egypt in haste"* (16:3). This unleavened bread possibly symbolized both their suffering in slavery and their hasty departure when God delivered them. Israelites who did not attend the feast apparently participated by removing all the yeast from their homes.

Think about how the Passover commemorated a historical event, when the blood of a lamb sprinkled on the doorposts of Israelite homes was a sign to "pass over" these protected homes. The death of the firstborn, which was judgment on the Egyptians, was avoided by this simple, but *essential*, act of obedience. Passover was to be a ceremony of remembrance (Exodus 12:24-27). Because they remembered all God had done for them in the past, they could trust Him for the future.

The principle holds true for us. We can keep in mind all that God has done for us and live in hope. In fact, sometimes looking back is the only thing that gives us the courage to look forward. When your world seems to be falling apart, *remember*. Remember how the Passover was perfectly fulfilled as Christ, the Lamb without blemish, shed His blood so God would not visit you with judgment and death, but would pass over you (Romans 6:23). Remember His gracious acts of love and mercy in the past, be encouraged in the present, and have courage and hope for the future.

The Feast of Weeks

The *"Feast of Harvest,"* or *"the day of the firstfruits"* was the second major festival celebrated annually. During New Testament times, Israel called this celebration *"Pentecost,"* reflecting the Greek translation of the 50 *days* between the first day of barley harvest and the end of wheat harvest. On the 50th day, sacrifices of animals and grains were more elaborate than those prescribed for the Feast of Unleavened Bread.

Moses instructed the Israelites to leave a portion of their grain at harvest *"for the poor and for the sojourner"* to glean (Leviticus 23:22). He directed Israel to consider giving to others as an important act of rejoicing and sharing, not as a rule or obligation. Those with plenty of food brought gifts to the celebration to share with those less fortunate. That way everyone could *"rejoice before the LORD"* (16:11).

The Feast of Weeks gained new significance on the day of Pentecost, 50 days after the Passover when Jesus died. The Holy Spirit's outpouring fulfilled God's promise (Joel 2:28-29) that He would pour out His Spirit on all people. Observing Pentecost today marks the initial proclamation of Christ's salvation message by Spirit-filled men and women.

Think about the two-fold significance of this festival. First, giving to God and to others should be *"in proportion to the blessings the LORD your God has given you"* (16:10, NIV). God does not want us to give what we do not have, but He expects that we will reflect His generosity toward us as we give generously to others. Second, when God's family gathers, no one is left out. Everyone was welcome at the festival, even foreigners in the land. The gracious giving during the Festival of Weeks foreshadows God's love and grace in the gift of His Son for all who believe (John 3:16). We respond to His grace with loving hearts and actions to those around us.

The Feast of Booths

The joyous Feast of Booths (or Tabernacles) occurred in the fall after dates, figs, grapes, and olives were harvested. The Israelites constructed booths (tents or huts) out of tree branches in their vineyards. The Lord promised He would meet them there and bless their produce and the work of their hands (16:15).

The Feast of Booths connected the celebration of God's gracious acts in Israel's history with thanksgiving for the present harvest. They had lived in tents for 40 years in the wilderness; they even heard the Law read to them out of a tent. They remember their history, so they will not forget that God is the sole source of Israel's existence and prosperity.

Personalize this lesson.

One of the trademarks of God's people is their joy and gratitude. God is good, and His people celebrate that goodness. What place does celebration have in your spiritual life? How can you cultivate more joy and gratitude? What specific goodness of God can you celebrate? Ask God to deepen the Holy Spirit's fruit of joy in your life. Then some time in the next month, find a way to express that joy in His presence and in the presence of His people.

Lesson 8

Leaders With Integrity
Deuteronomy 16:18-20; 17–18

Memorize God's Word: Deuteronomy 18:18.

❖ Deuteronomy 16:18–17:13—Godly Leaders

1. From 16:18-20, how were the judges and officers to judge the people, and why did God insist on this?

    _____

    _____

    _____

    _____

2. What three things are leaders told they must avoid?

    _____

    _____

    _____

3. According to verse 19, what effect does a bribe have?

    _____

    _____

4. Read 17:2-7. What is God's attitude toward people who worship created things rather than God, the Creator?

    _____

    _____

    _____

5. Read 17:8-13. Why is it important for Israel to comply with the Levites' and judges' instructions in legal matters?

_____

_____

❖ Deuteronomy 17:14-20—Considering a King

6. Moses foresees a time when the Israelites will want a king. What will be their reason for wanting a king?

_____

_____

7. List at least five instructions Moses gives to guide the selection of a king. Record at least one reason for each.

Instruction	Reason
1)	
2)	
3)	
4)	
5)	

8. Which of these instructions do you think is most important?

_____

_____

_____

❖ Deuteronomy 18:1-8—Caring for Leaders

9. How should the Israelites provide for the Levite priests? Why?

_____

_____

_____

10. What do you think is meant by *"the Lord is their inheritance"* (18:2)?

_____

_____

11. Do you think the Lord is your inheritance? How?

_____

_____

_____

❖ Deuteronomy 18:9-13—Abominable Practices

12. What are abominable practices in God's eyes?

_____

_____

_____

13. Review the Ten Commandments (Exodus 20:1-17). Which of these do the Canaanite practices listed in Deuteronomy 18:10-11 violate?

_____

_____

_____

14. How do you think Deuteronomy 18:9-13 applies today?

_____

_____

_____

❖ Deuteronomy 18:14-22—Concerning Prophets

15. How does a true prophet's work differ from how Canaanite diviners and fortune tellers did their work?

   _____

   _____

   _____

16. What principles for testing a prophet's words do you find in this passage? (See also 1 Thessalonians 5:19-22.)

   _____

   _____

17. Who do you think the *"prophet like me* [Moses]*"* (18:15) refers to? (See Acts 3:22-24.)

   _____

   _____

Apply what you have learned. *"Justice, and only justice, you shall follow, that you may live and inherit the land that the* LORD *your God is giving you"* (Deuteronomy 16:20). For *our own* sake, God demands that we practice justice. Our families, communities, nations, and world benefit when justice and righteousness are a customary part of our lives. Those of us who have the privilege of electing or appointing leaders should keep these traits in mind and exercise our privilege faithfully. And all of us should remember to pray for our leaders because even if they do not currently exercise these qualities, God can change their hearts.

Leaders With Integrity
Deuteronomy 16:18-20; 17–18

Israel's survival depends on her leaders being faithful, just, and true to God. Moses urges God's people to remain devoted to God alone in their worship, and offers instructions for Israel's leaders to maintain their integrity.

Godly Judges

Overwhelmed with the responsibility of judging all disputes, Moses had appointed men to mediate all but the most difficult matters, which he would decide (Exodus 18:13-26). Now he advises the Israelites to establish a similar justice system once they settle in the land. Every town will appoint godly individuals who will not pervert justice, show partiality, or take bribes. For Israel to survive as a nation, she must place people of integrity and character in these positions.

Living prosperously in the land depends on Israel's obedience to the covenant. Judges needed to decide cases based on God's standard of justice. They must not allow friendships to sway their decisions or accept payment from litigants who would likely influence their decisions. God plays no favorites. He does not want His chosen leaders to show favoritism either.

Think about how God expects us to reflect His character in the decisions we make. Leaders have an even greater responsibility because every abuse of power is an injustice to someone. Real wisdom is required to balance justice with mercy. You can support leaders who strive to reflect God's values through their actions. In God's eyes, we are responsible to pray for wisdom, discernment, and guidance for all leaders in our communities.

Kings in Israel

Moses anticipates that the Israelites will admire surrounding nations and want a king to rule them. Moses specifies that a king in Israel must be an Israelite *"whom the LORD your God will choose"* (17:15), and he must remain aware of his accountability to God. In addition, Israel's king must not accumulate horses, which represented military strength. Israel's strength was due to God's presence, and prohibiting a return to Egypt for more horses obviously discourages dependence on human efforts.

A king *"shall not acquire many wives"* (17:17). Normally, marriages to foreign princesses would strengthen a treaty with a neighboring state, but Moses had already indicated the danger inherent in such alliances. Now he cautions that the king's heart might be led away from Israel's true God. Israel has no hope for survival if a king loses sight of this essential truth.

A king *"shall not acquire … excessive silver and gold"* (17:17). Also, Moses indicated that a king needed to read and learn the Law in order to *"learn to fear the LORD his God"* (17:19-20) and avoid pride. Moses emphasized that God's Law was to be his lifelong companion and source of wisdom and strength. The standard for the king was the standard for all Israel.

Think about the prohibitions against future kings amassing horses, wives, and money. Horses represented the ability to conquer other peoples. Taking many wives to strengthen pacts reduced marriage to a political tool. God was their protection; they were not to depend on treaties with pagan nations. Accumulating fortunes implied reliance not on God but on themselves. Jesus promises us, *"Do not be anxious, saying, 'What shall we eat?' or 'What shall we drink?' or 'What shall we wear?' For the Gentiles seek after all these things, and your heavenly Father knows that you need them all. But seek first the kingdom of God and His righteousness, and all these things will be added to you"* (Matthew 6:31-33).

The Levites and Priests

God has chosen one tribe, the Levites, and set them apart to serve Him as priests in the tabernacle. Priests represent God to the people.

They explain God's standards and urge the people to obey His Law and commands. They also intercede before God with the people's pleas. Because the Levites *"shall have no portion or inheritance with Israel"* (Deuteronomy 18:1), God will provide for their needs through the people's generous giving. The tithes from all Israelites will be directed to the Levites *"for an inheritance, in return for their service"* (Numbers 18:21).

Think about Peter's words in 1 Peter 2:9: *"You are a chosen generation, a royal priesthood, a holy nation, a people for His own possession, that you may proclaim the excellencies of Him who called you out of darkness into His marvelous light."* While God chose the Levites to serve Him as priests then, all believers today are called to be a part of His priesthood. We are all gifted to serve Him in *"the work of ministry, for building up the body of Christ"* (Ephesians 4:12). Knowing God has chosen us as His ambassadors and worshipers, we can build each other up in love.

A New Prophet

Moses warns that different kinds of governments and spiritual practices will threaten Israel's future. God holds His people to a higher standard: *"You shall not… follow the abominable practices of those nations"* (18:9).

God promises to continue speaking to His people through a prophet like Moses. At Horeb, the people had been terrified by the thunder, lightning, trumpet blast, smoke, and fire—the visible manifestations of the Lord's presence. They had begged Moses to speak God's words. They feared that hearing God directly would cause them to die. After experiencing the genuine terror of God's nearness, they learn about His mercy through Moses. God has provided for His people and will continue to do so. He promises to raise up a prophet like Moses. Jesus Christ, the ultimate fulfillment of this promise, later told the unbelieving Jews, *"If you believed Moses, you would believe Me; for he wrote of Me"* (John 5:46).

Speaking of prophets in general, Moses later cautions that a prophet who presumes to speak things God has not authorized deserves the death penalty. A prophet's true character would emerge clearly as time revealed the truth or unreliability of his message.

Personalize this lesson.

Consider the godly leadership traits you studied in this week's lesson: integrity, dependence on God, single-heartedness, humility, commitment to God's Word. Ask God to help you evaluate which of these is most evident in your life and least evident. Ask Him to help you grow in the area in which you most need His help. That way, whether you are a leader already (most of us are, in some sphere or another) or will be in the future, you will be ready to lead well.

Covenant Renewal
Deuteronomy 27–28

❖ Deuteronomy 27:1-10—Last-Minute Instructions

1. Why is the authority of Israel's elders particularly important as Israel enters the land?

_____

_____

2. Why do you think Moses directs the people to write God's laws on large stones?

_____

_____

3. How would you describe their worship at God's altar?

_____

_____

4. Why are the stones and altar important?

_____

_____

❖ Deuteronomy 27:11-26—The 12 Curses

5. God will not tolerate behavior that violates His Law when the Israelites settle in the land. What sins does Moses specify?

_____

_____

6. What does the curse in verse 26 emphasize about the Law?

    _____

    _____

    _____

7. Why is it significant for everyone to respond, *"Amen"*?

    _____

    _____

    _____

❖ Deuteronomy 28:1-14—Obedience Leads to Blessings

8. According to Deuteronomy 26:16-19, how does the Lord view Israel?

    _____

    _____

9. How could you rewrite the blessings promised in Deuteronomy 28:3-6 in contemporary language?

    _____

    _____

    _____

10. Can you identify the verses in 7-13 that explain

    a) national security?

        _____

        _____

    b) economic security?

        _____

        _____

    c) spiritual security?

        _____

        _____

11. Which of these blessings do you find most significant personally? Why?

_____

_____

❖ Deuteronomy 28:15-57—Disobedience Brings Curses

12. Reread Deuteronomy 28:1-2, 15. What determines whether blessing or cursing occurs?

_____

13. Review your answers to question 12. What did Moses predict about each of the following?

    a) national security (Deuteronomy 28:32-33, 47-52)

    _____

    _____

    b) economic security (Deuteronomy 28:38-42)

    _____

    _____

    c) spiritual security (Deuteronomy 28:36-37)

    _____

    _____

14. How do you think Israel will respond to Moses' grim words?

_____

_____

❖ Deuteronomy 28:58-68—If ... Then

15. What do verses 58-63 reveal as more important to God than His people's comfort and prosperity?

_____

_____

_____

16. From verses 64-68, how would you describe the downward spiral that results from disobedience?

_____

_____

17. What is the final result of willful disobedience?

_____

_____

18. In one word, what is at stake if the people continue to disobey?

_____

Apply what you have learned. Deuteronomy 28 begins with the word "*if*." It implies a condition on which the well-being of a nation depends. It is not their "chosen-ness" that is in the balance—God has already chosen them. But their blessing is in question. If they obey God, their lives and their nation will be blessed. If they do not obey Him, they will miss out.

It's similar for us today. Our attitude toward God affects our well-being and the well-being of those around us. When we submit to God and love people, we will be blessed. That *could* include material blessing, but it will definitely include spiritual blessing. Consider how you have lived your life over the past three or four weeks. How has your heart attitude invited God's blessing? Are there any attitude changes you'd like to make? Talk with God about anything He reveals.

Covenant Renewal
Deuteronomy 27–28

God's people stand poised—ready to enter the Promised Land—and ready to become the settled nation God has long ago planned. Moses and the elders use this moment to relay last-minute instructions. Moses won't be crossing over the Jordan with them, and he realizes the importance of ensuring that Israel is fully prepared for the momentous task ahead.

Moses turns to blessings and curses in this passage. God's blessings may be immediate or delayed. In Numbers 6:22-26, Aaron and his sons blessed Israel: "*The LORD bless you and keep you; the LORD make His face to shine upon you and be gracious to you; the LORD lift up His countenance upon you and give you peace.*" Moses reminds the Israelites about what they must do to enjoy God's blessing, because the opposite of God's blessing is His curse. Moses tells this new generation about a covenant renewal ceremony they must perform soon after crossing the Jordan.

Last-Minute Instructions

Before Israel can enter the Promised Land, the people must gather large stones; then they must write "*all the words of this law*" on those rocks (27:3). They must build an altar where they can offer sacrifices, but they are not allowed to use iron tools to cut the stones. As God's people worship and rejoice, they will see His law displayed on these gathered stones.

When the Israelites enter the land, six tribes will stand on Mount Gerazim to hear the blessings. The remaining six tribes will stand on Mount Ebal to hear the curses. The Levites carried the ark of the covenant to the valley between the two mountains (Joshua 8:30-35). After the blessings and curses are proclaimed, everyone will respond "Amen" to reflect their agreement.

Biblical scholars are uncertain about why Deuteronomy 27 omits
the actual blessings. Perhaps emphasizing the curses rather than the
blessings appeals to the Israelites' sense of obedience. Meanwhile, the
12 curses specify the consequences for sinful behavior that may go
undetected by the public courts, but will not go unnoticed by God. The
12th curse summarizes Israel's responsibility to honor all of God's law as
part of the covenant renewal.

> **Think about** how the curses in verses 15-26 warn
> that the acts themselves negatively affect those who
> commit them. These sinful behaviors guarantee
> misery and destruction of their entire community's
> social fabric. Remember, God truly desires what is best for
> us. All His commands and prohibitions are designed to
> encourage good and harmonious lives. Our loving God
> would far rather reward than warn, bless than curse.

Obedience Equals Blessings

Moses reiterates that obedience brings blessings while disobedience
invites curses. The Canaanites still occupy the land, but Israel will go in
and take it despite the dangers. Moses reminds them that they will be
victorious, not due to their righteousness, but because of the Canaanites'
wickedness. Taking possession of the land will fulfill God's twofold
purpose: to judge the Canaanites and to give Abraham's offspring their
long-promised land. If the Israelites *"do all His commandments"* (28:1),
they will truly be *"a people holy to Himself"* (28:9). Other nations will
recognize God's blessing on Israel; they will highly regard Israel as she
makes loans, but never borrows, and remains economically strong. What
a remarkable promise God makes to a nation who has never experienced
owning land or running its own government.

Disobedience Brings Curses

Knowing that Israel's future depends on obedience to God, Moses
pronounces curses as a final warning about disobedience. *"If you
will not obey the voice of the LORD your God or be careful to do all His
commandments and His statutes ... all these curses shall come upon you
and overtake you"* (28:15). Moses cautions that forsaking God leads to

evil deeds. Israel, never victorious in her own strength, will swiftly fail without God.

Think about the voice of the Lord. Five times in this chapter, Moses warns about the importance of *"obeying the voice of the LORD of your God"* (verses 1, 2, 15, 45, and 62). *"Obeying the voice of the LORD"* leads to blessing, while failing to obey His voice leads to cursing. It is easy to become deaf to God's voice. We may become too busy to stop and listen. We may become distracted or confused by the conflicting messages we hear all around us. We may simply not want to hear. But not listening to God's voice is a serious matter. If we don't hear Him, we can't obey Him.

Moses now warns these former slaves about possible slavery for Israel in the future. Disobedience to God could lead to exile from Canaan and into a life of enemy domination as well as agricultural failure and economic instability. In fact, Israel will *"become a horror … and a byword among all the peoples where the LORD will lead"* them (28:37).

God wants His people to *"serve the LORD your God with joyfulness and gladness of heart, because of the abundance of all things"* (28:47). He had freed them from slavery, fulfilling His promise to bring them into Canaan's great abundance. But to receive God's blessing without joy or gratitude was to invite disaster. Moses urges Israel to remember and not forget all the things God has done. God's abundant blessing will continue if they faithfully obey His voice and carefully do what He commands (28:1).

Moses then contrasts the effects of obedience and disobedience. In the fullness of the covenant blessing, Israel will live a life of serving and loving God, enjoying the prosperity of the land. Under the curse, they will serve lifeless gods of wood and stone. Under God's blessing, other nations will fear Israel. Under the curse, Israel will return to where they will no longer be fit even to serve as slaves. It's hard to imagine a more graphic picture illustrating the consequences of obedience and disobedience.

Personalize this lesson.

✓ The land God designated for His people was neither large nor protected by natural barriers. It was a time-worn corridor used by armies that wished to avoid the desert to the east. Its fertility made it doubly enticing to outside nations. Yet this vulnerable land was the specific place God chose for His people.

Because He did not put them in an impregnable stronghold, it seems clear that His purpose was for them to trust in Him for their protection. God does not offer His people, then or now, a life securely walled off from mishap, danger, or struggle. God intends for His people to trust Him for their peace, protection, and provision. While wealth, might, power, people, jobs, or positions may provide a fleeting sense of security, they cannot keep us safe ultimately. Only God can do that.

What do you depend on for your security? Is there anything that hinders you from being able to trust God alone? Talk to Him about whatever He reveals. Confess any pride or independence. Confess any anxieties and fears to Him. Ask Him to help you live like the Psalmist did when he said, *"For God alone my soul waits in silence; from Him comes my salvation. He alone is my rock and my salvation, my fortress; I shall not be greatly shaken"* (Psalm 62:1-2).

Lesson 10

Choose Life
Deuteronomy 29–30

❖ **Deuteronomy 29:1-15—Standing Before God**

1. How does remembering past events give Israel the courage to move forward?

   _____

   _____

   _____

2. Moses emphasizes that the people are *"standing ... before the LORD"* in verses 10 and 15. Why are they gathered, and what sort of atmosphere do you picture?

   _____

   _____

   _____

3. What does it mean for us to stand in God's presence today?

   _____

   _____

   _____

❖ **Deuteronomy 29:16-21—Remain True**

4. What would you say is the root that produces bitter poison?

   _____

   _____

5.   What oath do you think is being referred to in verse 19?

_____

_____

6.   Why is it important for each person to remain true to God?

_____

_____

7.   What does this passage teach about the results of turning from God?

_____

_____

❖ Deuteronomy 29:22-29—Secret Things of God

8.   Refer back to 29:1, 9, 12-13. According to verses 22-27, what will receive the brunt of God's judgment?

_____

_____

9.   What actually happens to God's people?

_____

_____

10. Even in this most difficult scenario, what can we learn about God?

_____

_____

11. Referring to 29:29, what do you think are *"the secret things"* of God?

_____

_____

12. What are *"the things that are revealed"*?

_____

_____

13. How do these things lead to following *"all the words of this law"*?

_____

_____

_____

❖ Deuteronomy 30:1-10—Future Restoration

14. Why does Moses believe Israel will be restored?

_____

_____

15. What timeless encouragements are found in 30:1-4?

_____

_____

_____

16. What has changed between 10:16 and 30:6?

_____

_____

_____

❖ Deuteronomy 30:11-20—Choose Life

17. What does the word *live* in Deuteronomy 30:16 mean?

_____

_____

18. Why does Israel need to hear the encouragement in verse 11?

_____

_____

19. How can this verse encourage believers today?

_____

_____

_____

20. From verses 15-18, complete the chart about Israel's choices.

The choices available to Israel	The results of the choices
1)	1)
2)	2)

21. What do you choose, and why?

_____

_____

_____

_____

Apply what you have learned. Deuteronomy 29:29 allows us a sigh of relief. God does not require us to understand things above our comprehension. But neither does He excuse us from responsibility for things He has made abundantly clear. "*The word is very near to you*" (30:14). He means for that "*very near*" word to guide you to life. What "*very near*" word is being revealed to you? Think about this area of your life that God has made very clear to you. What can you do to make these words become part of your life?

Choose Life
Deuteronomy 29–30

Moses now focuses on the importance of the Israelites' decision as
they renew the covenant. Although the covenant renews the promise
made between God and His people at Horeb many years ago, it is new
for this younger generation. They are now ready to enter the land that
God denied the former generation because of their disobedience and
faithlessness. Renewing the covenant reflects the continuing relationship
between God and His people.

Standing Before God

Moses reviews God's acts throughout Israel's history. Despite His faithful
provision during their Egyptian slavery and their subsequent desert-
wandering years, Israel has failed to realize God's amazing favor toward
them. Israel's disobedience results in dulled perception. Moses longs
for them to come to a real understanding of God's ways. Everything
God had done was *"that you may know that I am the LORD your God"*
(Deuteronomy 29:6).

"Standing today ... before the LORD" (29:10), Israel agrees to renew her
covenant with God. Moses again warns about turning away from God
to idols, and he solemnly cautions that one individual or one tribe
turning to idolatry could affect the whole community. Sin has inevitable
consequences, which affect the innocent as well as the guilty. Anyone who
thinks, *"I* [will] *walk in the stubbornness of my heart"* is accountable to God
(29:19). God's anger will burn against him, and *"the curses written in this
book will settle on him"* (29:20). Remember, even God's patience has limits.

Moses predicts that God will allow calamities and diseases to afflict
Israel's land as punishment for her sin. Seeing Israel's land parched
and burned, nations will ask, *"What caused the heat of this great anger?"*

(29:24). The Israelites have broken God's covenant and have worshiped other gods. They have betrayed the total allegiance required in their covenant with God. Moses' warning was meant to encourage people to obey God, not frighten them into despair. Israel can avoid this terrible fate through obedience. Moses hastens to assure Israel that while God has not told them all His secrets, He has told them enough to enable them to follow His Law.

Keenly aware that the Israelites might persist in disobedience and fail in their obligations, Moses knows that God's judgment might be unavoidable. God has not given His people total knowledge. But what He does reveal should not be ignored. The Israelites could maintain a living relationship with God by following His Law. Understanding *"the secret things"* (29:29) is not essential; what is revealed is sufficient.

Think about two principles essential to Christian living contained in this passage. First, God has kept some things secret—we do not need to know them. If we did, He would have revealed them. Second, the revelation He has given is sufficient to enable us to live according to His will. This was true of Israel, and it is true for us. God forbids sorcery, witchcraft, and fortune-telling because they are attempts to gain knowledge apart from relationship with God. God has given us everything we need to know in order to obey.

Repentance and Forgiveness

Moses looks next toward future restoration. While God may scatter Israel because of her disobedience, Moses anticipates His forgiveness and restoration. He says Israel will *"return to the LORD your God, you and your children, and obey His voice in all that I command you today, with all your heart and with all your soul, then the LORD your God will restore your fortunes and have mercy on you"* (30:2-3). God will renew the ancient covenant, and the Israelites will be *"more prosperous and numerous than your fathers"* (30:5). Israel's history validates Moses' prophetic vision of the future.

Previously, God admonished Israel to act—to "*circumcise … your heart, and be no longer stubborn*" (10:16). Now God Himself promises to act—"*The LORD your God will circumcise your heart and the heart of your offspring, so that you will love the LORD your God with all your heart and with all your soul, that you may live*" (30:6). Obedience will lead to restored prosperity and God's renewed delight in His people. Although God moves believers' hearts, He does not force them to obey. The ultimate responsibility lies with them.

Think about how God does not turn His face away from repentant sinners. Time and time again, when Israel repented of her disobedience, God forgave and restored her. In the same way, God forgives us, repeatedly, when we turn to Him in repentance. David, who knew firsthand about God's grace and mercy, wrote a psalm about God's forgiveness (Psalm 103:10-13):

> *He does not deal with us according to our sins, nor repay us according to our iniquities. For as high as the heavens are above the earth, so great is His steadfast love toward those who fear Him; as far as the east is from the west, so far does He remove our transgressions from us. As a father shows compassion to his children, so the LORD shows compassion to those who fear Him.*

Choose Life

"*This commandment that I command you today is not too hard for you, neither is it far off*" (30:11). While it may seem overwhelming at times, it is not impossible to obey God's commands. Moses reminds God's people that the choice is theirs.

Moses eloquently states that Israel must choose between "*life and good*" or "*death and evil*" (30:15). With clarity, Moses has delivered God's Law. He has reminded the Israelites of their God-directed history, and he has presented their future possibilities. Israel is responsible to choose. The heart that turns to God prospers; the heart that turns away from God turns from His benefits. Moses pleads, "*Therefore choose life*" (30:19).

Personalize this lesson.

✓ God's people have clear alternatives: life and blessing if they remain obedient to God, death and destruction if they turn away. God's people could never plead ignorance of the Law or of consequences of wrong choices. They had choices—choices that mattered, choices with consequences—and they had the freedom to make them.

We also have choices to make—real choices, with real consequences. And God has told us everything we need to know to make the good choices. Moses said, "*Choose life*," and Jesus said, "*I came that they may have life and have it abundantly*" (John 10:10). Think about some of the choices you will make today, tomorrow, and the next day. Even seemingly unimportant decisions like how you handle your frustration or spend your time can lead to life or death for others and yourself. Always keep in mind the life that God intends for you. How can you make sure your choices lead to life? Ask God for help. He wants you to live! He will help you choose life.

Lesson 11

From Moses ... to Joshua
Deuteronomy 31:1–32:47

Memorize God's Word: Deuteronomy 29:29.

❖ Deuteronomy 31:1-13, 19-29—Leadership Transition

1. Why isn't Moses allowed to enter the land? (See Numbers 20:6-12.)

_____

_____

_____

2. How can you summarize Moses' attitude toward God, according to Deuteronomy 31:5-8?

_____

_____

_____

3. Who is Israel's actual leader? (Find quotes from Deuteronomy 31:1-13 to support your answer.)

_____

_____

4. As God's people, what are the Israelites supposed to do?

_____

_____

5. What do you think the Israelites may do instead?

_____

_____

❖ Deuteronomy 31:14-18, 23—Be Strong and Courageous, Joshua

6. Who is Joshua? (See Exodus 17:8-13; 24:13; Numbers 13:16.)

_____

_____

7. How will Joshua's previous experience enable him to lead Israel?

_____

_____

8. How does Moses encourage and support Joshua during this leadership transition? (Review 31:7-8.)

_____

_____

❖ Deuteronomy 31:19-22, 28-30—Introduction to Moses' Song

9. Whose idea is this song, and what is its purpose?

_____

_____

10. What will the people do in the land (31:20-22), and why?

_____

_____

❖ Deuteronomy 32:1-47—Moses' Song

11. What is Moses' attitude toward God in verses 1-4?

_____

_____

12. How do verses 5-6 indicate a change in the song's direction?

    _____

    _____

13. Which verses in 7-14 describe these three major events?

    a. Israel's election (being chosen) by God

        _____

        _____

    b. Israel's deliverance

        _____

        _____

    c. Israel's gift(s) from God

        _____

        _____

14. "*Jeshurun*" (Deuteronomy 32:15) is Israel's nickname, meaning *the upright one.* What do verses 15-17 state that Israel will do?

    _____

    _____

    _____

15. Why do you think Moses used "*Jeshurun*" in this passage?

    _____

    _____

    _____

16. Poetic *parallelism* is used in these verses. The first line makes a statement; the second (and sometimes more) expands and amplifies. Which couplet between verses 5-18 is your favorite, and why?

    _____

    _____

    _____

    _____

17. According to verses 19-27, what terrible things is God justified in doing?

_____

_____

18. According to verses 36-43, what does He actually do for Israel?

_____

_____

_____

Apply what you have learned. "*It is no empty word for you, but your very life*" (32:47). Take time this week to think about how different life would be if people throughout the world considered God's words to be words of "*life.*" Think how differently nations would interact, how safe neighborhoods would be! Then, think of your own life. If you took God's rules for life seriously, how would you treat others? How differently would you treat yourself? What is one change you plan to make this week in order to show that God's words are not empty, but are life to you?

From Moses ... to Joshua
Deuteronomy 31:1–32:47

The time has come. God chose Joshua to lead Israel into the Promised Land, and Moses is completing his leadership responsibilities. God protected Moses as a baby by ensuring that he would grow up in the Pharaoh's palace where he undoubtedly received extensive literary training and education (Exodus 1:8-2:10). Now Moses continues serving God as he records God's Law, commissions Joshua, and composes a divinely inspired song.

Moses Encourages Joshua and the People

Moses reminds the people how old he is and how he is unable to continue leading them. Calling Joshua to stand with him before the Israelites, Moses publicly assures and supports Joshua. *"Be strong and courageous, for you shall go with this people into the land that the* LORD *has sworn to their fathers to give them ... The* LORD *... goes before you. He will be with you; He will not leave you or forsake you"* (31:7-8).

Moses gave the Law to the priests and the elders, who would be responsible for publicly reading it every seven years so *"they may hear and learn to fear the* LORD *your God, and be careful to do all the words of this law"* (31:12). As each generation learned to fear and revere God, God's blessing would continue in the Promised Land.

Moses Commissions Joshua

God instructs Moses to take Joshua with him to the tabernacle where God reveals His presence in the pillar of cloud. Moses commissions Joshua to lead Israel. God then declares that His people *"will forsake Me and break My covenant that I have made with them"* (31:16). These tragic words introduce the song God wanted Moses to write and teach to Israel. By singing this song, the people would bear witness about the predictable consequences of unfaithfulness.

Think about how great leaders sometimes have to allow their people to fail. It must have been hard for Moses to hear God say that Israel would forsake Him and break His covenant. But Moses was a truly great leader. Rather than try to control and manipulate the people to bring about a better outcome, He trusted God for Israel's future.

In our desire to see our children (and others we feel responsible for) make good choices, we can become overprotective, domineering, or manipulative. Someone once said, "The secret of leadership is knowing when to take your hands off and trust the Holy Spirit to do the guiding." Just as we sometimes make foolish choices, so will our children also make poor decisions from time to time. But eventually each of us must assume responsibility for our own lives. We do a disservice to those we feel responsible for when we deny them personal accountability and delay their need to answer for their own behavior. Wise leaders will be faithful to the limits of their own callings, ask God to help discern what those limits are, and trust God to work beyond that.

The Song of Moses

As Joshua transitions into leadership, Moses recites the song to all of Israel. Moses' song eloquently includes advice and counsel (32:7, 28-29) as well as guidance about how to live (31:19). Moses reminds them that God is their reliable, permanent Rock (32:4) who rescues and preserves His children (32:10-11). God's generosity stands in sharp contrast to His people's ingratitude. The name *"Jeshurun"* (32:15) is Israel's nickname. Moses uses it in a negative way to emphasize Israel's lack of appreciation toward God. The *upright one* (Jeshurun) *"grew fat"* on God's abundance, but *"kicked"* as the people resisted God's love and control. (Notice that Moses speaks as if this future betrayal has already been accomplished.)

The Result of Israel's Idolatry

"I will hide My face from them" (32:20) graphically describes God's sorrow as He watches His children's sinful behavior and the disaster it invites. God is a jealous God; Israel's idolatry provokes His anger.

Think about the fact that God's jealousy is unlike human jealousy. The Israelites' lack of loving response to Him does not trigger feelings of inadequacy or personal abandonment. His concern is for them. Idols are not a threat to God (they would be no threat to Him even if they were real). The threat is for those who worship them. Jeremiah pointed out that people take on the characteristics of that which they worship: *"They went after worthlessnesss and became worthless"* (Jeremiah 2:5). God, knowing idols to be "no-gods," recognizes that His people will be lured away from His reality into spiritual emptiness. God, therefore, will severely discipline those who turn from Him to idols, so they might repent and return to Him. His jealousy is for *their* sake.

Instead of blessing them, God will *"heap disasters upon them"* as He fulfills the covenant agreement (32:23). The text implies that Israel is not paying attention. Moses delivers Israel over to the bleak consequence of her own actions. Moses even mentions Sodom and Gomorrah to show the disgrace Israel has brought on herself.

God's Vindication

Ultimately, God will settle the score with the enemy nations. When the Israelites' arrogance and attraction to foreign gods is totally demolished, God will demonstrate His compassion. Yahweh holds the power of life and death, sickness and health, and victory or loss in war. Death, disease, and defeat are all under God's power. *"I, even I, am He, and there is no god beside Me"* (32:39). He is the One who helps and shelters, wounds and heals, delivers into captivity and delivers out of captivity. He will avenge His people! After reciting this song with Joshua at his side, Moses says to all the people, *"Take to heart all the words by which I am warning you today. ... It is no empty word for you, but your very life"* (32:46-47).

Personalize this lesson.

✓ In these two chapters, we see again that God is serious about unfaithfulness. He knew the Israelites' willfulness and the patterns of their failure. *"They will turn to other gods and serve them, and despise Me and break My covenant"* (31:20). He warned them of the consequences of their unfaithfulness and the discipline they would receive.

God disciplines us, too, when we lose our way. Hebrews reminds us of how a loving father disciplines his children. God treats us in the same way. *"The Lord disciplines the one He loves. ... He disciples us for our good, that we may share His holiness. All discipline ... yields the peaceful fruit of righteousness to those who have been trained by it"* (Hebrews 12:5-11).

Think of a time when you made a bad choice and suffered painful consequences because of it. What did you learn from that experience? What did you learn about God? What has been the effect of God's discipline on your life?

Lesson 12

Moses' Blessing and Departure
Deuteronomy 32:48–34:12

❖ Deuteronomy 32:48–33:5—Moses and God

1. God reminds Moses, "*You did not treat Me as holy*" (32:51). How can we treat God as holy?

    _____

    _____

    _____

    _____

2. In 33:3-5, Moses alludes to the people's response to God. Using these verses and 32:39, what do you learn about God's attributes?

    _____

    _____

    _____

    _____

3. Which one of God's attributes that you mentioned in the previous question do you want to give more attention to or appreciation for? Why?

    _____

    _____

    _____

    _____

❖ Deuteronomy 33:6-17—Reuben, Judah, Levi, Benjamin, Joseph

4. Choose one or two words to describe the condition or hope revealed in Moses' blessing to these tribes:

    a. Reuben _____

    b. Judah _____

    c. Levi _____

    d. Benjamin_____

    e. Joseph_____

5. With which tribe do you most closely identify? Why?

    _____

    _____

    _____

    _____

❖ Deuteronomy 33:18-29—Zebulun, Issachar, Gad, Dan, Naphtali, Asher

6. Choose one of the blessings recorded in these verses, and translate it into contemporary language.

    _____

    _____

    _____

    _____

7. Which of these blessings would you most like to claim for yourself? Why?

    _____

    _____

    _____

    _____

8. What is Moses' tone as he concludes his blessing in verses 26-29? Record words or phrases that helped form your opinion.

    _____

    _____

    _____

    _____

9. Choose one of these verses, and share how you can apply it in your life.

    _____

    _____

    _____

    _____

    _____

❖ Deuteronomy 34:1-12—God and Moses, Moses and God

10. What are the phrases used to describe Moses in 34:5 and 10?

    _____

    _____

    _____

11. What do you conclude about the relationship between God and Moses?

    _____

    _____

    _____

12. Reread Deuteronomy 33:1-3 and 34:1-4. How would you describe Moses' relationship with God?

    _____

    _____

    _____

13. From the study of Deuteronomy, what strikes you as most admirable about Moses?

    _____

    _____

14. Which of Moses' qualities would you most like to possess? Why?

    _____

    _____

15. What have you learned about following God as you studied Moses' life?

    _____

    _____

    _____

Apply what you have learned. In the first Song of Moses are these words: *"Who is like You, O LORD, among the gods? Who is like You, majestic in holiness, awesome in glorious deeds, doing wonders? ... You have led in Your steadfast love the people whom You have redeemed"* (Exodus 15:11, 13). The song we have just studied, written at the end of his life, confirms that Moses never doubted that this is what God was like. Because he had a clear understanding of who God is, he was able to trust in the fact that God knew what He was doing. Moses' life ended at the precise time and in the precise way of God's choosing, and he died full of strength and full of faith.

How has God shown His power and glory in your life? Has He faithfully led you to this point? Choose to acknowledge and praise God for His care for you. Thank Him in your journal or share your thoughts about this with a friend or family member. We are His people and *"the apple of His eye"* (32:10). Rest in His encircling arms as you respond to His love with trust and obedience.

Moses' Blessing and Departure
Deuteronomy 32:48–34:12

Happy endings. Most of us long for them in our books, movies, and lives. At first glance, it almost seems as though Moses' life doesn't have the happy ending we all want for him. God excludes Moses from the Promised Land, and He allows Moses' successor, Joshua, to enter with the Israelites instead. Still, Moses is the man God knew face to face (34:10). In his deep disappointment, Moses continues to praise God: "*The eternal God is your dwelling place, and underneath are the everlasting arms . . . the shield of your help, and the sword of your triumph!*" (33: 27, 29).

God directs Moses to ascend Mount Nebo. From this peak, rising about 4,000 feet above the Israelite encampment, Moses would be able to see the Promised Land, which he was not permitted to enter. In this final blessing, Moses is "*the man of God*," a title used here for the first time in the Bible (33:1). Moses focuses Israel's attention upon the future, speaking of their life in Canaan as if it has already taken place.

Israel—the Family of God

Moses points to the greatest moment of God's manifestation in Old Testament times. God's revelation at Sinai was surpassed only in the incarnation of Jesus Christ. Three historical acts indicate God's authority as Israel's king: Israel's liberation (Exodus 15:19); God giving His Law at Sinai (Exodus 19 and 20); and the future victory God would give His people in Canaan (Joshua).

Moses Blesses Each Tribe

Reuben (33:6) Moses requests continuity for the tribe of Reuben, who was Jacob's firstborn son by Leah. Moses asks God to "*let Reuben live, and not die.*" Perhaps this hope is based on Moses' awareness of this tribe's volatile nature.

Judah (33:7) Moses asks God to grant Judah's prayer for military victory. Jacob had designated Judah as the royal tribe (Genesis 49:9-10), and under Moses, this tribe marched at the head of the army. This prayer acknowledges that God alone is the source of victory.

Levi (33:8-11) Neither Simeon's nor Levi's tribes would have their own land in Canaan, but they would have cities throughout the land where they could serve people as they brought their offerings to God. Because of their obedient willingness to execute judgment after the Golden Calf incident (Exodus 32:27-29), the Levites were appointed to oversee worship and religious education.

Benjamin (Deuteronomy 33:12) *Yahweh's* beloved dwells in safety and rests in God's affection and protection.

Joseph (Deuteronomy 33:13-17) Moses prays the largest of the northern tribes will prosper materially from the land's produce and militarily in war with other nations.

Zebulun and Issachar (33:18-19) Moses asks that their prosperity will prompt them to invite their fellow Israelites to join with them in thanksgiving to His abundance.

Gad (33:20-21) Moses blesses Gad for honorably leading God's people in how to fulfill His will.

Dan (33:22) Moses depicts Dan as *"a lion's cub,"* implying youthfulness with great future strength.

Naphtali (33:23) Moses prays for God's continued favor and the fullness of God's blessing.

Asher (33:24-25) Asher's tribe occupied the coastal land and was on the highway invaders used to reach Palestine. As a result, Moses prays for never-ending strength for this tribe.

Think about God's astonishing grace shown in Levi's appointment as the priestly tribe. (In the Hebrew mind, individuals were never considered apart from their clan or tribe.) Simeon and Levi, two of Jacob's sons, had deceived and killed the men of Shechem to avenge the violation of their sister, Dinah. Jacob bitterly condemned them: "*I will divide them in Jacob and scatter them in Israel*" (Genesis 49:5-7). More than 400 years later, his prophetic words were realized when neither tribe received territory of its own. Simeon received several cities within Judah's land, while Levi's descendants became priests, receiving cities throughout Israel's territory. God chooses, blesses, and directs in ways we would never envision, often working through those we may have thought unworthy.

Concluding Hymn of Praise

God's power is portrayed in His majestic passage through the heavens as He comes to His people's aid. They will find refuge and security in His presence, enveloped by His "*everlasting arms.*" Moses' long poem ends as it began, in praise of *Yahweh.*

Moses concludes by congratulating Israel: "*Who is like you, a people saved by the LORD*" (33:29). Viewed from the human perspective, Israel has little hope. But Israel can rejoice—even before entering the land—in the power of her incomparable God, who is her strength and will give her the victory over her enemies.

Moses' Departure

Instructed by God, Moses leaves his people and ascends Mount Nebo. From the Pisgah, which means *serrated ridge*, about 4,000 feet above the Dead Sea, Moses sees the vast panorama of the Promised Land, from Dan to the north on the lower slopes of Mount Hermon to the Mediterranean coast to the west and across the great rift valley of the Dead Sea to the south (34:1-3).

Forty years have passed since Moses first responded to God's call to lead His people to Canaan. Now God permits Moses, "*the servant of the LORD,*" to see the land—but not to enter it. Moses' death and burial were a private matter between him and his Lord.

The books of Exodus, Leviticus, Numbers, and Deuteronomy recount Moses' life. "*There has not arisen a prophet since in Israel like Moses, whom the LORD knew face to face*" (34:10). These words confirm Moses' unique position among all other leaders in Old Testament times. With God's help, Moses liberated the Israelites from Egypt, mediated the covenant with God, and brought God's Law to Israel.

Personalize this lesson.

☑ The Israelites were a difficult people to lead. Fickle, grumbling, rebellious—they were hardly the kind of people who would have been easy to bless. However, when Moses was about to die, he chose to speak words of encouragement and affirmation over them. He chose to bless these people who had so many times been a thorn in his side.

Do you bless people? Even those who seem unworthy? What difference might your words of encouragement mean to someone who struggles? Who knows how many men and women and children have failed to achieve great things because someone withheld encouragement and blessing from them. Will you choose to live the rest of your life as one who intentionally blesses others and calls out God's best in them?

Small Group Leader's Guide

While *Engaging God's Word* is great for personal study, it is generally even more effective and enjoyable when studied with others. Studying with others provides different perspectives and insights, care, prayer support, and fellowship that studying on your own does not. Depending on your personal circumstances, consider studying with your family or spouse, with a friend, in a Sunday school, with a small group at church, work, or in your neighborhood, or in a mentoring relationship.

In a traditional Community Bible Study class, your study would involve a proven four-step method: personal study, a small group discussion facilitated by a trained leader, a lecture covering the passage of Scripture, and a written commentary about the same passage. *Engaging God's Word* provides two of these four steps with the study questions and commentary. When you study with a group, you add another of these— the group discussion. And if you enjoy teaching, you could even provide a modified form of the fourth, the lecture, which in a small group setting might be better termed a wrap-up talk.

Here are some suggestions to help leaders facilitate a successful group study.

1. Decide how long you would like each group meeting to last. For a very basic study, without teaching, time for fellowship, or group prayer, plan on one hour. If you want to allow for fellowship before the meeting starts, add at least 15 minutes. If you plan to give a short teaching, add 15 or 20 minutes. If you also want time for group prayer, add another 10 or 15 minutes. Depending on the components you include for your group, each session will generally last between one and two hours.

2. Set a regular time and place to meet. Meeting in a church classroom or a conference room at work is fine. Meeting in a home is also a good option, and sometimes more relaxed and comfortable.

3. Publicize the study and/or personally invite people to join you.

4. Begin praying for those who have committed to come. Continue to pray for them individually throughout the course of the study.

5. Make sure everyone has his or her own book at least a week before you meet for the first time.

6. Encourage group members to read the first lesson and do the questions before they come to the group meeting.

7. Prepare your own lesson.

8. Prepare your wrap-up talk, if you plan to give one. Here is a simple process for developing a wrap-up talk:

    a.   Divide the passage you are studying into two or three divisions. Jot down the verses for each division and describe the content of each with one complete sentence that answers the question, "What is the passage about?"

    b. Decide on the central idea of your wrap-up talk. The central idea is the life-changing principle found in the passage that you believe God wants to implant in the hearts and minds of your group. The central idea answers the question, "What does God want us to learn from this passage?"

    c. Provide one illustration that would make your central idea clear and meaningful to your group. This could be an illustration from your own life, or a story you've read or heard somewhere else.

    d. Suggest one application that would help your group put the central idea into practice.

    e. Choose an aim for your wrap-up talk. The aim answers the question, "What does God want us to do about it?" It encourages specific change in your group's lives, if they choose to respond to the central idea of the passage. Often it takes the form of a question you will ask your group: "Will you, will I choose to … ?"

9. Show up early to the study so you can arrange the room, set up the refreshments (if you are serving any), and welcome people as they arrive.

10. Whether your meeting includes a fellowship time or not, begin the discussion time promptly each week. People appreciate it when you respect their time. Transition into the discussion with prayer, inviting God to guide the discussion time and minister personally to each person present.

11. Model enthusiasm to the group. Let them know how excited you are about what you are learning—and your eagerness to hear what God is teaching them.

12. As you lead through the questions, encourage everyone to participate, but don't force anyone. If one or two people tend to dominate the discussion, encourage quieter ones to participate by saying something like, "Let's hear from someone who hasn't shared yet." Resist the urge to teach during discussion time. This time is for your group to share what they have been discovering.

13. Try to allow time after the questions have been discussed to talk about the "Apply what you have learned," "Think about" and "Personalize this lesson" sections. Encourage your group members in their efforts to partner with God in allowing Him to transform their lives.

14. Transition into the wrap-up talk, if you are doing one (see number 8).

15. Close in prayer. If you have structured your group to allow time for prayer, invite group members to pray for themselves and one another, especially focusing on the areas of growth they would like to see in their lives as a result of their study. If you have not allowed time for group prayer, you as leader can close this time.

16. Before your group finishes their final lesson, start praying and planning for what your next *Engaging God's Word* study will be.

COMMUNITY
BIBLE STUDY

Million+ people are engaging with God and His Word through CBS

Community Bible Study (CBS) is a global, interdenominational Bible study ministry offering a wide range of courses exploring various books of the Bible in both written and spoken formats, for all ages. Currently available in more than 85 languages, CBS Bible studies impact lives across more than 110 countries worldwide.

Since 1975, CBS has served as a conduit for the transformative power of God's Word; our participants study the Bible together in diverse settings, such as churches, prisons, schools, refugee camps, homes, coffee shops, and on the Internet. CBS is a participation-based ministry with trained leaders who foster in-depth, holistic engagement with God's Word within the context of a caring community, both in person and online.

The vision of Community Bible Study is, "Transformed Lives Through the Word of God."

The mission of Community Bible Study is, "To make disciples of the Lord Jesus Christ in our communities through caring, in-depth Bible Study, available to all."

CBS makes every effort to stand in the center of mainstream historic Christianity, concentrating on the essentials of the Christian faith rather than denominational distinctives. CBS respects different theological views, preferring to focus on helping people know God through His Word, grow deeper in their relationship with Jesus, and be transformed into His likeness.

Are you ready to go deeper in God's Word?

We would love to have you join us for an in-person or online CBS group. Scan the QR code to find a group.

For more information call 1-719-955-7777 or email info@communitybiblestudy.org.

Engage Bible Studies are available from Amazon and fine bookstores near you.

Scan the QR code to see all the available titles.